Case Studies in Educational Technology and Libary Leadership

Steven M. Baule

Professional Development Resources for
K-12 Library Media and Technology Specialists

Library of Congress Cataloging-in-Publication Data

Baule, Steven M., 1966-
Case studies in educational technology and library leadership/Steven M. Baule.
    p. cm.
Includes bibliographical references and index.
    ISBN 1-58683-153-4 (pbk.)

1. Educational technology – United States – Case studies. 2. School library media centers – United States – Case studies. I. Title.

LB1028.3.B383 2005
371.33--dc22

2004023411

Published by Linworth Publishing, Inc.
480 East Wilson Bridge road, Suite L
Worthington, Ohio 43085

Copyright ©2005 by Linworth Publishing, Inc.

All rights reserved. Purchasing this book entitles a librarian to reproduce activity sheets for use in the library within a school or entitles a teacher to reproduce activity sheets for single classroom use within a school. Other portions of the book (up to 15 pages) may be copied for staff development purposes within a single school. Standard citation information should appear on each page. The reproduction of any part of this book for an entire school or school system or for commercial use is strictly prohibited. No part of this book may be electronically reproduced, transmitted or recorded without written permission from the publisher.

ISBN: 1-58683-153-4

5 4 3 2

Table of Contents

Introduction .... *i*
    A Framework for Addressing Leadership Issues   *v*

Chapter 1: Censorship, Copyright and Accountability *1*
    The Filtering Follies   *3*
    Muggles, Muggles Everywhere   *7*
    Well, That Isn't Education Related!   *13*
    Mr. Warlick's Videos   *17*
    Oh Those Phone Bills   *21*

Chapter 2: Equipment and Software Issues *25*
    What Size Is Your Screen?   *27*
    To Buy or Not to Buy   *31*
    The Downloading Blues   *35*
    To See or Not to See   *39*
    A New Car for the Information Superhighway   *41*
    Passwords or Spot123   *43*
    Needful Things in the Athletics Office   *45*
    The Vanishing Vendor   *49*

Chapter 3: Managing People *55*
    A Favor for the Boss   *57*
    Motivating and Retaining Technical Staff   *61*
    Skills or Else!   *67*
    The Managers' Ultimatum   *71*

Chapter 4: Instructional Issues *75*
    Computer Course Requirement   *77*
    Absentee Teachers in the Labs and Libraries   *81*
    Going to School at Home?   *83*
    Block Scheduling in the High Schools   *85*
    Typing to Graduate   *87*

Chapter 5: Library Programming *91*
    Your Job Is on the Line   *93*
    To Build or Not to Build: That Is the Question   *97*
    Library Degree Not Required   *101*

Chapter 6: Planning and Program Evaluation *105*
    The Accountant-less Audit   *107*
    The White Elephants   *111*
    Creating a CIO   *113*
    Assessing Your Own District   *121*

Chapter 7: Additional Issues for Discussion *123*

Chapter 8: Considerations for Resolving the Cases *135*

Index *153*

This book is dedicated to the love of my life, Kathy, who puts up with my strange desire to write and to my Sydney and Sam who are always willing to help by pushing the computer's keys.

*Deliberations are always about means,
not about ends*
— Aristotle, Nicomachean Ethics

Educational technology is surely one of the largest growth areas in schools today. In fact, it would be hard to find a school today that does not utilize technology to support direct instruction, to provide electronic information resources, and to support administrative functions. One of the first ways computers entered schools was through the school library media centers. Today computer and network technologies have become permanently intertwined with the traditional library media programs of the 1970s and 1980s. This has caused a great deal of change and a few challenges among school library media professionals and educational technologists. Some traditional library functions, such as the need to advocate intellectual freedom, however, remain unchanged, at least in principle.

These professionals work in constantly changing environments and often have not had formal training to address the issues they are confronting. Universities are often just not able to keep up to date with the myriad of changes going on in K-12 education. In the best of cases, the technology coordinator or the school library media specialist can call on his or her colleagues to ask how others handled similar situations. This text is an attempt to provide educational technology and school library media professionals an opportunity to review the facets of potential issues before they confront them on the firing line of everyday work. Likewise, the text will provide an analysis of the facets that need to be considered in addressing any technology related issues in an educational setting. The attempt of this text is to provide a holistic view of how to address educational technology issues and to provide practical cases in which to practice those analytical skills.

Case Studies as a Teaching Method

In 1986, Vivian Clark promoted the use of case studies for aspiring principals. She articulated that case studies were an effective methodology for training principals and other educational administrators. Clark articulated that case studies stimulated students to share techniques and promote a dialogue among the participants that other methodologies could not (Clark, 1986). Today, case studies are a common part of many educational administration and other leadership and management programs. Case studies have moved into secondary education as well under the term problem-based learning. A wide variety of case study information is now available for educational administrators. However, few if any of the extent materials touch on the complex and fluid worlds of education technology and library media programs.

The purpose of case methodology is two-fold. It can be used to teach new information and theories in context, in much the same way as literature-based instruction is used to teach language arts skills in context. This allows instructors to provide students an opportunity to see how espoused theories can be used in practical situations. In many such situations, a particular case can be reviewed after the introduction of a management theory or other tool or set of tools that would be particularly suited to the issues set forth in the case. This use of the case method tends to support the leadership as science perspective. Given the right tools, the solution or solutions to a problem can become readily apparent.

A second use for case studies is to teach the transference of skill sets students already possess. In these cases, the student is encouraged to adapt to a potentially new situation relying on their current professional skills and experiences. According to many adult learning theorists, and constructivist theories in general, exercises that require learners to adjust their current paradigms to new situations is one of the best ways to teach. Using case studies in this way is particularly effective as it allows experienced learners, as most educators are, to have their previous experiences and skills validated or challenged. Especially when used as prompts in cooperative or other group work, case studies can help experienced educators, as well as pre-service educators, recognize that all professionals will not respond the same to given situations. Such learning is an excellent way to teach adults and obtain a higher degree of participation in the activities. This use of the case method tends to support the leadership as an art point of view. Together the two uses of the case methodology can be a powerful method of instruction.

Case studies also have the advantage of providing a more participatory learning environment that provides for a more engaged student. This environment facilitates critical thinking, reflection, and effective problem-solving skills that could not be as easily developed in other methodologies. Case studies encourage teamwork and accountability. The realism of case studies is also a motivator to adult learners. (Barnes, Christensen, & Hansen, 1994; Tomey, 2003).

Types of Case Studies

According to Matejka and Cosse, case studies used to teach come in three types; true cases, disguised cases, and fictional cases. (Matejka & Cosse, 1981). True cases are presented as they originally occurred. These cases use the actual names of the participants and organizations involved. Military case studies tend to follow this rule. The efforts of Colonel Joshua Chamberlain at Gettysburg's Little Round is an example of a true case study often presented to aspiring U.S. Army officers. Disguised cases are similar to true cases in that the situations did actually occur. However, the names and occasionally exact circumstances have been altered to obscure the identity of the participants. These cases are similar to the cases displayed on television police drama like *Dragnet* or *Law and Order*. The third type of case is the fictional case. These cases are created to illuminate potential leadership or management situations. Many simulation software programs provide this type of case study. In such programs, the computer allows you to manipulate a variety of variables around a given scenario. The cases in this text are generally disguised cases.

Teaching with Case Studies

When using case studies with students or when reviewing them as an individual, the following things should be kept in mind. The first is that the purpose of the case study is to bring a small "chunk of reality" into view for the learner. These cases are based upon actual problems that another professional educator had to deal with. In this way, case studies are one of the ways to closely approximate on-the-job training.

The second issue is that, just as in a real situation, all of the information you might want to have about a situation is not available. Managers are not omnipresent and able to know the entire details of any given situation. In the same way, creating an effective case study requires that one has enough information to articulate one or more possible courses of action, but not too much information as to make one course of action seem the only option. One must remember there is more than one "right answer" for each of these cases. For each case, any number of potential courses of action might present themselves. The key in determining a course of action or a recommendation is to be able to justify one's position grounded in a combination of theory and experience.

Steps to Facilitate Reflection and Discussion

Several methods can help you work through a case study. The following have been articulated for those working with cases. One of the best ways to begin is to follow the heuristic below.

> 1) *Determine the primary issue to be addressed. In some cases, there will also be secondary problems that, although not as compelling, will also need to be addressed.*
>
> 2) *Articulate the known facts in the case. Then review the facts to ensure that all of them are germane to the issues identified above. Ignore information that is not pertinent to the issue(s) at hand.*
>
> 3) *Identify potential courses of action.*
>
> 4) *Conduct any necessary research to ensure that the courses of action are viable options.*
>
> 5) *After the research has been done to confirm the validity of the courses of action, enumerate the strengths and weaknesses of each potential course of action.*
>
> 6) *Select a course of action and provide the necessary support, both theoretical and practical, to back up your decision.*
>
> 7) *Discuss how various changes in the case may have affected your decision of a course of action. What other information would one liked to have had? What information was the most compelling in making a decision? What information was not important to the case?*

Case studies can also be reviewed through a specific individual's perspective. One could also address a given case through the lens of a specific organizational or management theory.

A Framework for Addressing Leadership Issues

Courses of action should be weighed in how they impact different facets of the school. These areas generally consist of the following:

- *Curricular and instructional impact*
- *Personnel issues for both student and staff including collective bargaining*
- *Facilities impact and related issues*
- *Fiscal impact and related issues*
- *General governance including policy and procedure management, legal issues, and ethics*
- *Public relations including the civic impact and any potential impact on other educational organizations*
- *Technological impact*

Today, our schools and society as a whole are so enmeshed with technology, that technology weaves itself throughout nearly all of the facets articulated above. Technology, however, is often considered as a stand-alone facet of a problem, if it is considered at all. In fact, technological issues run through most of the strands and are particularly interdependent with facilities issues.

Curriculum and Instruction

In the area of curriculum and instruction, the key is to determine a course of action's potential impact on the teaching and learning process. As educators, the issues brought up under curriculum and instruction are often the focus of new initiatives. However, it is important to be able to take a wide view of how these issues may impact all other areas of a curriculum. Often, especially in larger districts and comprehensive high schools, the present balance of the curriculum is a delicate one. Adding a technology course requirement may end up destroying an elective art program due to scheduling problems.

As education is the business of schools, this needs to be the primary focus of weighing the impact of various courses of action in most situations. Will the school be able to provide a better academic product if this course of action is implemented? Will teachers be able to teach with fewer impediments and be able to spend more time on pedagogical issues as opposed to administrivia, etc.? Are the instructional goals supported directly or indirectly? Will this course of action help provide graduates who are prepared for their future life experiences?

Personnel

In many situations, personnel issues are probably the most complex. Considerations regarding personnel issues need to have a dual focus. The first focus is that of student impact. How will this course of action potentially impact students individually and collectively? If it impacts graduation requirements, will current students be grandfathered? How will it potentially affect student service functions within the school or district? Will the course of action have an equitable impact on all students regardless of socio-economic status or other stratifications?

Regarding staff impact, the same issues apply. Will the impact be the same on all types of staff? Will one subgroup be more impacted than others? Will the course of action be in compliance with any existing collective bargaining agreements? Will a course of action impact morale either positively or negatively? Will the course of action have an impact on the ability to recruit or retain certain types of staff? Considerations for staff development will also need to be addressed at this point of the decision making process as well.

Facilities

Can the course of action be followed within the existing building? Will there need to be any physical improvements in order for the course of action to be successful? Are there enough classrooms? Computer labs? Does adequate power and data infrastructure exist to support a new course of action? For instance, in deciding to provide an electronic point of sale system in the cafeterias throughout the district, did one consider the existing power and data locations in the cafeterias? Will the new computer lab's equipment generate so much heat that the HVAC systems will have to be modified?

Fiscal

At the simplest level, how much will the course of action directly cost? Few courses of action can be analyzed at that level. Often there are indirect costs including staffing, training, etc. The total cost of ownership for the system should be reviewed. However, in most schools, the money could be found to fund any given course of action if it were the district's greatest priority. What other projects or programs could potentially be eliminated to make room for this course of action? If funding is limited, could the course of action be implemented incrementally? Could a user fee be attached to the project?

Governance

Does the course of action work within the existing framework of laws, school codes, policies, and procedures? Will the course of action potentially put the school or district into a position to violate any laws or its own policies? Will more senior administrators be able to support the course of action given past practice and similar practices in other areas of the school? Similarly, the ethical and professional constraints of a potential course of action should be considered as part of this facet.

Public Relations

Public relations are often a key concern in determining a course of action in education. Public schools are particularly a public trust and the community's view of a school's reaction to a situation can have long term consequences in either a positive or a negative direction. How will the community react to a give course of action? Will they support the change? Is the issue able to be reduced to simplest terms for the general community? Will the explanation be understandable for most citizens?

In private schools, the issue becomes even more paramount as such schools rely on parents, alumni, and other donors to provide much of their funding. They need to be particularly careful in managing potentially difficult situations. If a school decides not to filter its staff computers, will the community look at that as having to support teachers surfing the net at taxpayer or donor expense?

The last piece of this facet is to review how a course of action is in line with what other schools or districts are doing. If you are going to take a course of action that is extremely divergent from other practices in the area, state, or even nationally, will that divergence play a roll in the success or failure of the course of action?

Technology

In determining a course of action, there are a number of common facets that need to be considered in nearly all technology related issues.

- *Access to Technology*
- *Comfort and Ease of Use*
- *Interoperability*
- *Standardization*
- *Reliability and Support*

Depending upon the particular issues of a given situation, some of these facets will weigh more strongly than others. In some cases, one or more facets will not be germane at all. However, in most cases each of these facets will need to be considered.

Access

One of the most important facets of any educational technology decision is what kind of access it will provide to end-users. Student access must be considered as well as staff access. Most studies that address the achievements of successful technology programs articulate that wide and open access is paramount to success. Access can be as simple as providing the right number of computers in a classroom or as complicated as ensuring the right levels of network file or system access are available for specific staff roles when those staff members remotely connect to the school's network. Generally, access issues are not easily determined as they need to be "just right" to paraphrase Goldilocks. Too little or too great of access are equally poor choices.

Comfort and Ease of Use

Does the solution proposed have the look and feel of existing software? Does it work through a Web-like interface or does it work only through a command line interface? Will users, either students or staff, be able to easily transfer their present technology skills and knowledge to using the new program or system? If not, will there be a steep learning curve as users learn the new system? Will users dislike the new system and will that cause unnecessary grief and disruption during a transition. If students have similar systems at home, that will help ease any transition.

Interoperability

Does this implementation of technology interact and work with existing systems. New systems need to work with the currently installed base. Maintaining multiple systems and bridging between systems that do not interact is difficult and time consuming. Examples of basic interoperability include the SIF project to ensure educational related administrative systems can exchange data. At a more basic level, will the new software program run on the operating system(s) used in the school?

Standardization

The issue of standardization is a critical one for technology. Unlike many other areas of education where staff often have wide latitude in implementing programs or curricula, technology requires a level of system-wide standardization not common in many educational settings. All technology issues need to be considered within the context of existing school or district standards. Technology leaders need to ensure that a course of action does not move away from standardization unless the benefits of such a move strongly outweigh the advantages of maintaining standards.

Reliability and Support

Will the course of action provide for a system that is reliable and supportable? Some systems might be possible, but the fragility of a system may make it an unrealistic proposition for a school to be able to support such a system. If the system is particularly complicated or takes an extremely high level of training to maintain it, it may not be supportable within the district. If a particular course of action will require reliance on long term outside consultants for minor or even moderate system issues, the course of action would be less practical than one that would allow internal staff to support the system.

The Cases

This text provides cases that are intended to provide realistic situations that could occur in schools and districts. In fact, in one form or another, these issues all have faced educational leaders. These cases have to be addressed by the educational technology or school library media leadership in the school or district.

Each case provides an introduction to the school and district. Within these background descriptions, there are some key points one should take into consideration when determining a course of action. Often, as in real life, there will also be information that is extraneous to the question or questions presented. In some cases, the exact nature of the question may need to be decided upon before one can proceed.

After providing the background, the case will either provide a specific problem or an assignment from a superior in the district. These assignments are generally clear, but as with real life supervisors, there is occasionally room for interpretation within the problem or assignment. As in real life, being able to articulate one's perspective of the issue is often as important as determining the potential solution.

In some cases, one will also be given additional information provided by one's invisible colleagues or others involved in the case. In nearly every case, there are also some potential resources available for your review depending upon what one has determined are the main points to be resolved in the case. In no case is the listing of resources to be considered exhaustive. One should feel free to find as many additional resources as they deem necessary to support their proposed course of action.

For some of the cases, potential solutions have been provided as examples. They should not be considered as dogmatically correct. They are simply the best response of practicing educational technologists and library media specialists. They are provided so one has something to compare his or her own answers with. They should not be considered as being the "best answer." In military leadership, the answer often varies under the phrase, "the terrain dictates." Similarly, in educational leadership, the individual culture of the school or district may have a dramatic impact on how one leads. So there is no one "right answer" for any of the cases presented here. However, in all of the cases, there are facets of the case that must be addressed.

References

Barnes, L.B., Christenson, C.R. & Hansen, A.J. (1994). *Teaching and the case method.* Boston: Harvard Business School Press.

Clark, V. (1986). The effectiveness of cases studies in training principals, using deliberative orientation, *Peabody Journal of Education, 63*(1), 187-195.

Jones, D.C. & Sheridan, M.E. (1999). A case study approach: Developing critical thinking skills in novice pediatric nurses, *The Journal of Continuing Education in Nursing, 30*(2), 75-78.

Kowalski, T.J. (1991). *Case studies in educational administration.* New York: Longman.

Matejka, J, & Cosse, T. (1981). *The business case method: An introduction.* Richmond, VA: Robert F. Dame.

Tomey, A.M. (2003). Learning with cases, *The Journal of Continuing Education in Nursing, 34*(1), 34-38.

Chapter 1

Censorship, Copyright, and Accountability

The Filtering Follies

Description of the School District and Community

Gibson City is a small semi-rural community with a population of 20,000. Approximately 2,500 college students attending Martin Luther College inflate this number during the academic year. Gibson City's primary industry outside of the college is a large meat packing plant that draws a great number of commuters from the smaller villages and farms in the area. The temperament is an unusual mix combining the traditional Midwest small town conservatism while still supporting the open intellectualism of the college and its faculty. Church attendance is still high in Gibson City and the clergy are leaders in many aspects of community life. The college faculty members are generally highly regarded as leaders within the community. The current school board is made up of two college faculty members, the spouses of two ministers, a retired teacher, an accountant, and a retired farmer.

The Gibson City Schools serve Gibson City itself and a number of the smaller surrounding communities. The district includes seven small elementary schools, two middle schools, and a single high school. The schools are fairly autonomous in nature with each principal providing its direction. At the high school, teachers are given a great deal of academic freedom in emulation of the freedoms held by the college faculty. Many of the high school faculty members have spouses or significant others working at the college. So there is a great deal of interaction between the two faculties.

The Background

Several years ago, the district began to filter Internet traffic in compliance with the Children's Internet Protection Act. The faculty was generally opposed to any kind of filtering, but the technology director simply pushed the need to comply with the law, and filtering was implemented for students. The IT staff braced for an onslaught of complaints from teachers whose students were unable to access needed sites for research, but no such complaints appeared. The occasional request for a specific site to be unblocked was always accommodated in a timely manner. In fact, the opposite happened. Teachers started to complain that the filters were not blocking enough sites, so those sites were usually added to the filtering lists.

However, staff computers remained unfiltered. Over the course of several years, more than a dozen staff members were suspended or terminated for misuse of technology. Most of these cases were simple cases of perusing pornography over the Web. However, some were more serious including one teacher who was soliciting prostitutes through e-mail. As the district administration reviewed a number of IT related policies, the superintendent decided she wanted to filter all computers including staff machines. A number of staff members complained that this would affect their ability to conduct research on a variety of topics including such things as breast cancer and hate groups. Other teachers simply expressed frustration that they were no longer trusted as professionals.

The Assignment

As you are the instructional technology director for the district, the superintendent and her cabinet have asked you to articulate responses to the following questions from the teachers' union:

- *What impact will this have on students and teachers researching debate topics such as weapons of mass destruction?*
- *How will this filtering affect access to personal ads, e-Bay, etc.?*
- *Will staff members still be able to conduct online banking, book airline trips, etc.?*
- *What will the administration be monitoring about staff technology use?*
- *What can staff do if a site they need to access is blocked?*

Additionally, the cabinet has asked you to recommend a course of action as to whether or not to filter staff machines. If you choose to filter staff computers, would you also recommend filtering the dial-up access that the district provides for staff from home?

Potential Resources

Ardito, S. C. (2002). *New filtering and censorship challenges, Information Today,* November 1.

Buchanan, L. (1999). *New filtering and censorship challenges, Multimedia Schools, May.*

Filteringinfo.com (2003). *Internet filtering legislation information. Available at* http://www.filteringinfo.org/.

N2H2. (2003). *Sites blocked by Internet filtering programs. Available at* http://cyber.law.harvard.edu/people/edelman/mul-v-us/

Oder, N. (2002). *Filter law doubted in schools, Library Journal,* October 15.

Wilson-Smith, A. (2001). *Here's the news you can't have, Maclean's,* July 9.

Muggles, Muggles Everywhere

Description of the School District

The Seaside Community School District is in the southwest. The communities served by the district are fairly conservative and nearly Bible Belt in their moral orientation. The number of retirement villages and active adult communities in the area are on the rise. A large Hispanic population is growing as well. Nearly 40% of the citizens in the area speak Spanish at home. Nearly 60% of the students in the district are Hispanic. A large number of white children are home schooled. A home schooling organization has worked hard to obtain regular access to the school libraries and computer labs in the district. The community has generally been supportive of the school district. This is partially due to the recent concessions of the district towards the home schoolers with regard to library and computer lab access.

Due to some key retirements and some poor hiring decisions, the district has been through a fair amount of recent turmoil and administrative turnover. The district has had three superintendents over the past four years and is presently under the direction of an interim superintendent. Due to that turmoil, the district has not updated any of the board policies over the past few years. In addition, some of the policies appear to have expired due to one of the superintendent's desire to have each policy only be effective for three years to ensure its timely revision. However, that superintendent resigned after only six months on the job. Similarly, the superintendent's secretary left for a job in a more stable district, so nearly 10% of the district's policies are effectively null. The district's policies on instructional materials including the library selection and reconsideration policies are among those policies that expired.

The Background

Two of the home school mothers using one of the middle school library media centers with their children were disturbed to find that three of the Harry Potter books were in the media center collection. They immediately took the books to the library media specialist and demanded that they be removed from the collection. The library media specialist was so taken aback and slightly in shock that he went to the principal. The principal was brand new and agreed to take the books off of the shelf. One of the home school moms identified herself as the sister of a school board member which half terrified the principal.

The district library media director has refused to remove the Harry Potter titles from all of the other library media centers. The parents responded by gathering over 1,000 signatures to remove the titles from all of the school's library media centers. At least four of the seven board members are leaning toward supporting the removal of the titles. However, several of the board members are hoping that the district staff can ensure that the right process is followed in determining whether or not to remove the young wizard from the schools. A number of the board members do not want to follow the expired board policy simply because another expired policy was ruled as having expired and having no standing by a local court. They are afraid using the previous policy would be opening them up to an appeal in court.

The Assignment

The superintendent comes to you as the technology director and a former library media specialist, to chart the proper course of action and make a recommendation to the whole Board of Education as to the proper process to follow. The superintendent also provides you with several items that he feels may help you in making your recommendation.

The Previous Policy for Reconsidering Instructional Materials

Request for Reconsideration of Instructional Materials

The Seaside Community School District welcomes comments and suggestions regarding the continued appropriateness of materials in the collection, especially concerning outdated materials. Suggestions will be considered and utilized by the staff in the ongoing process of collection development.

Individuals may take issue with instructional materials that do not support their tastes and views. Staff is available to discuss concerns and identify alternate materials that may be available. If a patron's concern is not satisfied through discussion with staff, a formal, written request for reconsideration of materials may be submitted to the school principal or school library media specialist.

No materials will be knowingly added to the school's collections that have been previously determined to be in non-compliance with local laws. The citizen submitting the request must be a resident of the district. The district will respond in writing, within thirty days of receipt, to the citizen's request for reconsideration. The response will indicate the action to be taken and reasons for or against the request.

Since a challenge is a highly emotional issue, the Board and staff have developed a step-by-step procedure in the case of a material challenge at the Seaside Community School District.

The following procedure will be followed.

1) *Any material(s) being challenged would be pulled on the receipt of a written challenge.*

2) *If found to be relevant and complete, the principal would hold the book for the challenge committee in order of: chair, oldest serving to newest member.*

3) *The challenge committee as individuals would read and complete a challenge form, returning the material with the challenge form to the director who would check out the material to the next person on the hold list.*

4) *Then the material with copies of all the challenge forms would be given to a staff member who would provide the defense of the material in an open meeting of the board, with recommendations of the challenge committee.*

5) *The board would then have a recorded vote on the retention of the materials. This accomplishes several objectives:*

   • *It keeps the material in circulation until it has been adjudged.*

   • *It removes the material from being stolen by some "defender of the faith".*

   • *It assures that Board Policy is followed.*

6) *Finally the board's decision is final, unless instructed by a court to do otherwise. If the materials are "lost," replacement materials will be purchased until a final determination by the Board is made.*

Deselected materials will be dealt with as per policy.
Approved by the Board of Education on July 17, 2000. To expire June 30, 2003.[1]

---

[1] Based on the selection policy available from the Northeast Iowa Library Service Area.

The Selection Policy of Another Area School District Library Program

GENERAL STATEMENT

The purpose of the Kaskaskia Library Media Program is to serve the needs of the school. Materials are therefore selected to support the curriculum and the mission of the school, to help each student develop his/her potential as a human being, and to help each teacher to achieve his/her professional goals.

The Kaskaskia Library Media Program endorses the American Library Association's Bill of Rights as interpreted for school library programs and the Association for Educational Communications and Technology's Statement on Intellectual Freedom.

SELECTION AND EVALUATION OF MATERIALS

Materials will be selected by qualified personnel, relying heavily on reviews found in standard reviewing media. Library media specialists will try to provide a balanced collection of the highest quality in which students can find a variety of points of view on curriculum-related topics, along with standard works in fields covered in the curriculum and quality works on subjects of current interest.

Librarians will select on the basis of principle and reason rather than personal opinion and prejudice. Recommendations from the school community are welcomed and encouraged.

Staff members involved in selection of resource materials will use the following criteria as a guide:

- *Educational significance*
- *Contribution the subject matter makes to the curriculum and to the interests of the students*
- *Favorable reviews found in standard selection sources*
- *Favorable recommendations based on preview and examination of materials by professional personnel*
- *Reputation and significance of the author, producer, and publisher*
- *Validity, currency, and appropriateness of material*
- *Contribution the material makes to breadth of representative viewpoints on controversial issues*

- *High degree of potential user appeal*
- *High artistic quality and/or literary style*
- *Quality and variety of format*
- *Value commensurate with cost and/or need*
- *Timeliness or permanence*

CONTROVERSIAL MATERIALS

The major areas of controversial materials for this school are sex, politics, and religion. A sincere effort is made to find materials covering contrasting points of view, especially in the area of politics and public issues. Materials on religion are chosen to explain rather than convince, and are selected to represent the field as widely as possible for school purposes. In a literary work the use of profanity or treatment of sex is not an adequate reason for eliminating the material from the school library. In general, materials should be selected for their strengths rather than eliminated for their weaknesses.

RESPONSIBILITY FOR SELECTION

Responsibilities for selection will rest with appropriate professionally trained personnel who will discharge this obligation consistent with the Kaskaskia Library Media Program's adopted selection criteria and procedures. Selection procedures will involve representatives of the professional staff directly affected by the selections, and persons qualified by preparation to aid in wise selection.

PROCEDURES FOR SELECTION OF LEARNING RESOURCES

In selecting learning resources, professional personnel will evaluate available resources and curriculum needs and will consult reputable, professionally prepared aids to selection and other appropriate sources. Among sources to be consulted are:

- *Bibliographies (latest edition available, including supplements)*
- *Current reviewing media*
- *Other sources will be consulted as appropriate. Whenever possible, the actual resource will be examined.*

Selection is an ongoing process that should include the removal of materials no longer appropriate and the replacement of lost and worn materials still of educational value.

GIFTS/DONATIONS

We reserve the right to use gifts at the discretion of the librarians. They may be donated to a more appropriate organization. Gifts that will be useful additions to the libraries will, of course, be added to the collection.

Potential Resources

American Library Association. (1996). Library Bill of Rights. Available at http://www.ala.org/ala/oif/statementspols/statementsif/librarybillrights.htm.

American Library Association (2003). Challenge support. Available at http://www.ala.org/Content/NavigationMenu/Our_Association/Offices/Intellectual_Freedom3/Challenge_Support/Challenge_Support.htm.

Banks, S. (1990). Schools winning more censorship fights, The Los Angles Times, Aug. 30, 8.

Hopkins, D.M. (1993). Put it in writing: what you should know about challenges to school library materials, School Library Journal, 39(1), 26-30.

Keokuk Community School District. (2003). Reconsideration of instructional materials policy. Available at http://www.keokuk.k12.ia.us/middle_school/mediacenter/reconsideration_policy.htm.

Internet Public Library. (2003). IPL materials reconsideration policy. Available at http://www.ipl.org.ar/about/ifpol.html.

No telling what my mother doesn't know. (2003). American Libraries. 34(8), 17.

Northeast Iowa Library Service Area. (2003). Model reconsideration policy. Available at http://www.neilsa.org/consulting/XYZ/reconsider.html.

SLIP. (2003). School library information portal. Available at http://www.cla.ca/slip/standards.htm.

Well, That Isn't Education Related!

Description of the School District and Community

First Star Community School District is a medium sized district with approximately 1,000 students in five school buildings. It is in a suburban area and the schools are strongly supported by the community. The community is generally conservative. The district employs 124 staff members of all types. Each school has computers in most classrooms, but some of the computers are more than five years old. Each school has a centralized software inventory and all computers have monitoring software on them. However, only student machines are filtered when accessing the Internet.

The teachers' union has an excellent working relationship with the administration. This creates a truly professional atmosphere and morale is generally excellent. The teachers are ordinarily given a great deal of freedom and rarely questioned as to how or what they teach. Each teacher has signed an acceptable use policy (AUP) agreement upon being hired. More experienced staff signed the AUP when computers were connected to the Internet.

The Problem

As you finish working with a teacher on a PowerPoint project, your network manager comes into your office and closes the door. One of your repair staff was responding to a run of the mill help desk call for help with a graphics program. He found that the graphics program had been confused by having documents saved in an irregular directory. That directory also included a number of pornographic files.

After Further Investigation

Your staff has determined that the teacher in question had over 4,500 pornographic files on his computer. Included within these files were no images of obvious child porn. However, many of the files were of a hardcore nature. In addition, it was obvious through e-mail and browser logs that the teacher had been setting up group sexual encounters through his school e-mail address. Topping all of this off, it appeared that the teacher had borrowed from the school's AV department to videotape some of his sexual encounters. It does not appear that either his office mates or any of the students were aware of his porn habit. All teachers have unique logins and passwords and all of the items found were clearly linked to his account and password. The materials date back over four years. The teacher in question had signed an AUP. The AUP clearly articulates that all use of the school's network must be used for educational use only and are not to be used for personal use. The teacher has tenure.

The Assignment

After gathering the evidence, you meet with the assistant superintendent for personnel. He agrees with you as to the seriousness of the situation. However, you also both agree that the teacher will need to be given due process. He has to go to another meeting and does not really understand technology. He wants you to outline the next steps that the administration should take and to articulate how mitigate the potential arguments that he might make that the items are not his.

Review this situation with the context of the acceptable use policy of your local school district and any collective bargaining agreements that might be pertinent. If you do not have an AUP in your school or district, decide what policy, if any, the employee might have broken.

Potential Resources

Searching the Internet under acceptable use policy should bring back a wide number of policies to review.

Acceptable Use Policies from Armadillo (TX) School District
http://www.rice.edu/armadillo/acceptable.html.

BitPipe IT White Papers. Available at http://www.bitpipe.com.

Kilpatrick, I. (2003) Stop snooping on your employees. Available at http://www.itsecurity.com/papers/wick4.htm.

Sex, Censorship and the Internet. Available at http://www.eff.org/CAF/cafuiuc.html.

Other Questions:

- *What if the teacher argues that he had forgotten about the AUP restrictions? It had been so long since he signed it? What could you do in the future to limit that argument?*

- *How would you respond to an argument that the teacher's privacy was violated when you went through the logs on his computer?*

- *How would you respond to the Union's potential argument that if the school did not want teachers to access pornographic materials they should have filtered such sites? By not filtering such sites under CIPA, the district is guilty of negligence and therefore the teacher cannot be held accountable for accessing information that the school should have limited.*

- *How would you react if the information indicated that the teacher was involved in paying for sex?*

Mr. Warlick's Videos

Description of the School

The Ashland Middle School has approximately 975 students and 48 faculty members in a suburban location. The majority of the faculty has been in the school for more than ten years and are generally viewed as recalcitrant by the district office, at least in the context of new programs and initiatives. You are the new library media specialist/technology coordinator for the school. You are new to the district. You remember that in the interview process, the district technology/media director, Mr. Elmo Hines, emphasized the need to follow copyright law and that he felt that was an area of concern in some parts of the district. You report directly to the building principal, Ms. Jane Swisher, who is less concerned about the specificity of the legal aspects of the job, but is very interested in getting teachers to use the library resource center more than they have in the past.

The library media specialist that you replaced, Mrs. Emma Gone, was interested in supporting teachers in any way she could. She was popular with the teachers but last year, she announced she was moving to another city to follow her husband to a new job. Across the street is an elementary school. The elementary school library media specialist/technology coordinator, Diane Reader, has been appointed as your mentor. She has been in the district for about a dozen years and is fairly familiar with most aspects of the district. She is strongly supportive of Mr. Hines. The AMS school computer teacher, Mr. Jon Martinez, is effectively in "on the job retirement." He is regularly sick and has not offered any help to you in your new position. You have two aides, a library clerk, Mrs. Cathy Griffin and a computer aide, Mrs. Carrie Summers. Both seem to enjoy working with you in the first weeks on the job.

One of the highlights of the Library Resources Center (LRC) is a large group presentation area with a wide screen television purchased a couple of years ago by the Parent-Teacher Association. The area is used for most faculty meetings and can hold about 2½ classes. The library collection is about 8,000 volumes including over 600 videos.

The Background

You have been in the building for about a month when Carrie comes to you with a problem. She has been asked to continue taping a PBS science program each morning for one of the 7th grade science teachers, Mr. John Warlick. Mrs. Gone used to tape the shows in case one of the teachers wanted the show. Yesterday, Mr. Warlick's outside lessons were thwarted by a rainstorm, so he came into the LRC looking for the tapes and was frustrated when they were not available. He had yelled at Carrie about not taping them and then found another video and stomped off.

In addition, Carrie also reported something you suspected, that the vast majority of the video tapes, over 400 were taped off air and not purchased. In some cases, two or three videos are on a single tape. The teachers use the video collection fairly regularly and it was something Mrs. Gone was proud of. Carrie recently began taking graduate courses in educational technology and her teacher recently covered copyright issues in class. Carrie is looking to you for guidance.

The advice you are given:

- *Jane Swisher tells you to do the right thing, but does not provide any additional guidance that is helpful.*

- *Elmo Hines feels that anything that violates copyright rules should be immediately destroyed and any inappropriate practices stopped immediately. Diane Reader is very supportive of Mr. Hines's views.*

- *Cathy Griffin suggests that the teachers will revolt if the videos are removed and that Ms. Swisher does not like the boat rocked. A number of the most respected teachers in the school are frequent users of the video collection.*

The Problem

Outline the issues involved, including any legal issues that may need to be addressed. Then articulate what steps you would take in the situation and how you would hope to resolve the issues.

Potential Resources

California student media and multimedia festival.
Available at www.mediafestival.org/downloads.html.

The crash course in copyright.
Available at www.utsystem.edu/OGC/IntellectualProperty.

Copyright Web site. Available at www.copyrightwebsite.com.

Crews, K. (2001). Copyright essentials for librarians and educators. Chicago, American Library Association.

Friends of active copyright education. Available at http://www.csusa.org/face/.

Groton (CN) Public Schools. (2003). Copyright implementation manual.
Available at groton.k12.ct.us/mts/cimhp01.htm.

Library of Congress. (2003). United States Copyright Office. Available at www.loc.gov/copyright/.

Microsoft copyright use of images.
Available at www.microsoft.com/permission/copyright/cop-img.htm.

Ten myths about copyright.
Available at www.templetons.com/brad/copymyths.html.

Walth, L. (2002). Adventures in understanding the jungle of copyright laws, Computers in Libraries. May, 16.

Oh Those Phone Bills

Description of the School District

Henry Stephens School District is an affluent suburban school district just north of a major metropolitan area. The district is comprised of four schools. Three elementary schools of approximately 500 students each form the elementary half of the district. Stephens Jr./Senior High educates the 1200 students in grades 7-12. In total, the district has nearly 500 employees. The district has a very strong teachers' union and its teachers are among the highest paid in the state. However, the district is starting to see a strong enrollment increase and the budget, which in the past has always been very flush, is being strained as more students enter the district. In the past, funds were always present for any project that had merit. The future will be different and the culture of Stephens may have difficulty adjusting. The school board members, the majority of which are new, are demanding a higher level of accountability. They have asked the superintendent and principals to figure out ways to cut costs without eliminating any important programs. This has created a great deal of angst among the teaching staff. One teacher even brought in a pack of poster board and lathe and left them outside the teachers' lounge to signify the extreme unhappiness that the faculty feel about the anticipated cutbacks.

The Background

In the first round of "cost containment conversations" several staff members mentioned that their peers regularly abuse the phones in the buildings. Currently, each teacher and counselor has an individual computer and telephone in his or her classroom or office. The telephones have never been limited as to accessing long distance or informational calls. One of the reasons for this has been that so many parents work in different areas codes within the tri-state metropolitan area.

The district does have a specific telephone policy in place stating personal calls should be less than five minutes in duration and should not be regular occurrences during the school day. Long distance calls are to be charged to personal calling cards and not charged to the district. This policy, however, is generally ignored. In a quick check of the district spends nearly $1,200 per month on 411 calls.

The teachers' union has said that limiting the present access to telephones would be a change in working environment and would have to be bargained. They have said that since the policies regarding telephone use have been routinely ignored by the administration, they are effectively not in place. When the high school principal reminded her department chairs that the telephones were not to be used for personal long distance calling, more than one department chair was aghast that anyone would monitor their personal use of the telephone. Another chair commented that he didn't think his teachers knew they shouldn't use the phones for personal calling.

In speaking with the telephone vendor for the district, a number of options were presented. Currently, the district is running through four separate telephone systems. The district office shares with the high school and each elementary school has its own system. However, these systems do not work together. You have to dial the entire 11-digit number for any person outside of your school. The vendor recommends either consolidating to a single traditional PBX system or migrating to an IP Telephony solution. As each building is completely networked, the IP telephony system would be able to be implemented without additional wiring costs. He also spoke to the fact that you could limit 411 calling options and long distance options by requiring a PIN number.

The associate superintendent also asked you to look into the possibility of integrating faxing into the system and allowing her to check her e-mail via the telephone. The superintendent has also mentioned that any services that are limited will still need to be available to the staff in some manner. However, those current telephone services may need to be replaced with free services.

The Assignment

Therefore, the business manager has been directed to work with you to figure out ways to contain telephone costs and hold staff members more accountable. Since the business manager has a number of other reports to complete, he is leaving this in your lap. You need to articulate the following:

- *How to handle long distance access and accountability*
- *How to handle information (411) access*
- *Any other considerations you feel are important*

Potential Resources

Cisco Systems (search for "telephony") (2003). Available at http://www.cisco.com.

4 Point Technologies (2003). (A consulting company to assist in selecting telephone systems). Available at http://www.4pointstech.com/callcenters.htm.

Lindström Telia, J. (2001). New ways of using video telephony. Available at: http://www.stakes.fi/cost219/videotelephony.htm.

The Link Wireless Telephone System in K-12. (2003). Available at http://www.bitpipe.com/data/detail?id=975725941_445&type=RES&src=av_reports.

Also search under "selecting telephone systems," "education and telephony" and similar search terms.

Chapter 2

Equipment and Software Issues

What Size Is Your Screen?

Description of the School District

The Brenton School District is relatively small serving 650 students K-12 in two school buildings located in rural Illinois. The schools are connected to a WAN for Internet connectivity and educational systems, but still rely on phone lines for the administrative systems. The district has about 400 computers throughout the schools including one computer for each of the 55 teachers. The district has a decent funding structure for technology but like many rural districts, it is always short of funds. The district is standardized on using MS Office. Each building has a computer technician and a library media clerk in place along with a district librarian/technology coordinator, Sydney Otting.

Brenton is a very conservative area and was originally founded by French Jesuits in the 1700s. The community recently went through a very difficult teachers' strike and the School Board took a tremendous beating in the weekly paper. Since then, the Board and the administration have been under very tight scrutiny. Teachers are regularly letting the paper's editor know about "things at the high school."

Computers within the district have always been strictly standardized Apple Macintoshes. Recently, the district has gone to leasing its one-piece Macs. Printers, scanners, etc. are all available in rationed numbers throughout both buildings. Each teacher has their own classroom as well except for the French teacher who moves between both buildings.

The Background

Christina Cheri is one of the district's most difficult teachers. She was previously the union president and is generally a negative person. Her principal, a former science teacher, refers to her as the electron, since she is always negative. Most of the time, she avoids any contact with the district's administrators and is always the last one into the high school in the morning and the first to leave at the end of the day. She teaches the honors and AP English courses. Although she is not a very good teacher, she is adequate with students who are motivated and don't need a lot of extra help.

When the district moved to a 4x4 block schedule a few years ago, she nearly herniated at a Board meeting ranting about how the students would all fail and become disciplinary problems with 85 minute periods. In fact the district's graduation rate and college placement rates are both up and are partially attributed to the block schedule. Someone regularly leaves a building block on her desk. She feels that the administration is doing it since no one has been caught yet. She has also regularly complained that the district should be using Windows computers instead of Apples. She feels all colleges use Windows machines so we should as well. In fact, her husband sells computers at Brenton's only computer store. So she has a vested interest in selling Windows computers. In general, Christina is not a coworker with whom anyone wants to have to work.

As the present school year is about to start, Christina delivers a doctor's note to her principal. It identified that Christina has poor eyesight and needs a larger computer monitor. She offers that a 21" screen will allow her to use the computer without the serious headaches and eyestrain she suffers from.

The principal and Sydney Otting explain to her that her computer monitor's resolution can be changed to default to a more magnified image. However, she responds that if she did that, she would have to scroll back and forth to see an entire page at once. She feels that she should not have to do that since other staff members don't. She ends with a rather heated, "This is a reasonable accommodation, and I deserve it after 28 years of faithful service to the district. I would hate to have to file a grievance." Christina then leaves the meeting.

The Assignment

Later, Sydney calls you asking for help. You are the technology coordinator for the area's special education cooperative. Sydney asks you what she should do. Does the district really have to provide her a larger monitor? If so, does it have to be a 21-inch monitor? Are there other options using assistive technology? What can you tell her? She needs to respond to the superintendent and the Board of Education. As Sydney hangs up the phone, she utters "Help! This lady is driving me nuts!" You have always gotten great support from Sydney, so you go to work to answer her questions.

Potential Resources

Job Accommodation Network. (2003). ADA hot links and document center. Available at http://www.jan.wvu.edu/links/adalinks.htm.

Microsoft. (2003). Types of assistive technology. Available at http://www.microsoft.com/enable/at/types.aspx.

United States Government. (2003). DisabilityInfo.gov. Available at http://www.disabilityinfo.gov.

Also search the Internet using the terms ADA and assistive technology. Also identify any local or state ordinances that might apply.

To Buy or Not to Buy

Description of the School District and Community

The Hinsdale Community School District is rather small by suburban standards, serving only 1,200 K-12 students in three buildings. The secondary school serves grades 7-12 with about 600 students. The two elementary schools each serve about 300 students. The district's test scores are always at the top of the state tests each year. The district is the kind in which everyone would like to work and few people leave except for an occasional administrator who is off to a superintendency. The communities served are all white-collar bedroom communities with income levels far above the median levels in the state. The property taxes are high, but they pale in comparison to the costs of private schools in the urban center. Effectively, the residents of the district are paying a premium for the wonderful schools they have access to.

The district employs over 300 staff members of all types. Although there are significant differences in salaries between the teaching staff, the classified support staff and the building custodial staffs, the district has always tried hard to treat all employee groups similarly. The professional development programs have always been open to all, and custodians and paraprofessionals have been in classes next to veteran teachers learning to use the computer and other technology. Even training in creating Web pages and similar high-end training was just as available to the secretary making a page for her grandchildren as for a chemistry teacher making a page to explain lab procedures.

The district, it seems, has always been this way, and experienced staff members refer to it as the "Hinsdale family." Retirement speeches and similar events nearly always refer to the family atmosphere of the district and the cafeteria workers are feted in the same manner as retiring administrators. Some newer staff find the family atmosphere to be in name only, but they play along and smile when the old timers refer to family atmosphere or the "unique culture" of the schools.

The Background

The business manager, however, is new to the district and has little of the family spirit. She is generally focused on nothing but the bottom line. As the director of technology, you are one of the few administrators who was not promoted from the district's teaching ranks. She has come to you to question everything from the annual sweatshirts provided as Coaches' Day gifts to the amount of food provided for administrative meetings.

This time she is calling you to ask about the computer purchase program that has been offered each year for all staff. The purchase program has been little more than a no interest loan to staff to purchase a computer. In the past, any staff member could obtain up to $3,000 to purchase hardware and software for their own use. The loan was paid back through payroll deduction over two years. The technology purchase did have to be for their own use, but it is commonly known that staff with children about to go to college nearly always purchased a new computer. In addition, many of the staff members who did not use computers at work including custodial staff and security personnel purchased computers each year.

The business manager feels that these expenses are extravagant. She wants to limit the funding of computer purchases to only be for certified staff. She doesn't feel the classified staff need to have school-financed computers for their home use. When she brought this issue up at the weekly administrative team meeting, the majority of the administrators were confused as to why it would not be open to everyone. She stated that she felt that only teachers were legitimately using computers at home to complete district work, so only they should have access to the computer purchase program. She also stated she didn't think that peripherals besides printers should be included. She felt digital cameras, etc. were more likely personal items and not professionally necessary.

The Assignment

The superintendent closed the discussion quickly and asked you to review the purchase policy and make a recommendation as to whether or not all staff should have access to the program. He wants to hear your response at the next weekly cabinet meeting.

Right after the meeting, several of your colleagues offer to support you if you recommend allowing all staff to avail themselves of the program. One or two administrators comment about how the custodians really do not need computers at home and that the teachers should be served first. The business manager's assistant reminds you that the business manager has taken a school computer home for her own use and demanded you provide new one for her last year. They all wish you luck in putting together your recommendation.

When you explain your assignment to the network administrator, he flips out, since he was planning on purchasing a computer this year through the purchase program to replace his old computer. Since he is not a member of the teaching staff, under the business manager's proposal, he would not be able to participate. Your secretary is also upset, but she just tells you the business manager doesn't value anyone but herself anyway.

Additional Information – The Past Process

In the fall, staff members were required to bring in the specifications for the computer they wished to purchase. Then the Director of Technology approved the specifications as meeting the district's standards. The staff members then brought in a receipt and received a lump sum check to cover that amount. Beginning January 1, the business office started to collect the loan through payroll deduction over the next two years.

Potential Resources

Bartholomew (IN) Consolidated School Corporation (2001). Instructional technology update: Guidelines for purchasing a home computer. Available at http://www.bcsc.k12.in.us/docstechnews/tu0111.htm.

CNET. (2003). What to look for in desktops. Available at http://reviews.cnet.com/4520-3118_7-5021315-1.html?legacy=cnet.

Hastings and Prince Edward District School Board. (2003). Suggested home computer purchase specs. Available at http://hpedsb.on.ca/ec/its/homespec.htm.

Internet Public Library. (2003). Pathefinder: Purchasing a home computer. Available at http://www.ipl.org.ar/ref/QUE/PF/buycomputer.html.

Paideia School. (2003). Suggestions for purchasing a home computer. Available at http://www.paideiaschool.org/tech/purchasing.htm.

Sayerville (NJ) Public Schools. (2003). Technology. Available at http://www.sayrevillek12.net/technology.htm.

Additional Questions

- *How might your response to the superintendent change if the business manager was to explain that over the past several buy programs, custodians have purchased computers and then returned them as soon as they had the purchase approved for reimbursement? In effect, they ended up getting a 24-month interest free loan from the school district.*

- *What if you found out staff that left the district never ended up paying their loans back? Would that change your response to the superintendent?*

- *In some cases, the staff members would bring these computers into the school to have the district IT staff repair them. They held the expectation that since they had purchased them through the school, the school district was responsible for their upkeep. Would that change your response to the superintendent?*

The Downloading Blues

Description of the School District

The Moonrift Community School District is relatively large serving 8,200 K-12 students in eight school buildings located in the state's industrial belt. The schools are each connected to a basic WAN infrastructure for Internet connectivity and educational systems, but still rely on phone lines for the administrative systems. The district has about 3,500 computers throughout the eight schools. There is a mixture of PCs and Macs in each building. The district has a decent funding structure for technology, but it needs a better overall plan about how to provide for continuing support of technology. The district is standardized on using MS Office at the elementary schools. The staff development program has been nothing more than your basic smorgasbord approach. About half of the teachers are active technology users with a higher percentage at the elementary level. The district has a typical administrative software program, and the elementary schools use phone lines to connect to the secondary school where the MIS systems are located. Each building has a single technician in place with a pair of network staff at the high school.

The community itself is fairly conservative. Moonrift is not that far from the Bible Belt. The community holds the teaching staff in high esteem and expects them to be model citizens. A few years ago, public outcry forced an unmarried elementary teacher to leave her third grade teaching position when she became pregnant. The teacher chose to move out of the area instead of enduring the stress of public exposure. About 15% of the school age population is home-schooled at the elementary level.

The Background

Technology has been a slowly evolving entity in Moonrift; there is a drastic lack of standardization or policy in place throughout the district. Computers began to arrive in small clusters where individuals, teams, or departments decided what they needed and how the technology would be used. Over time, these same individuals and small groups networked their computers to improve access to printers and eventually to provide Internet access. Some departments added servers to share data or manage printing services.

When the district began to provide for school-wide computing and district-wide infrastructure, the legacy systems were incorporated into the mix including the self-maintained high school science department server on AppleTalk and the peer-to-peer Windows server in the primary wing of one of the elementary schools. So, those staff members who were early adopters had significant freedom to maintain their own systems, install software, edit preferences, etc.

In the past year, the district's data processing manager and network manager have worked to remove all of the legacy systems[2] and provide the same functionality via district-wide systems. However, a number of teachers, department chairs and administrators have demanded that they retain control over their desktops and a few local servers.

Some student machines have some local desktop security software installed on them, but due to problems with desktop layout software it was removed from the art, newspaper, and yearbook computers at the high schools.

That access has created a system rife with viruses and illegal copies of software. Many computers are down due to incorrectly installed utilities programs, screen savers, and such executable files as the Dumb Ass Bass. At the same time, some teachers need to have access to install software that they brought in from home or bought for their class. They don't feel that the IT department can install these software programs in a timely manner. In some cases, the teachers want to use the software they bought last night in class the next morning.

The Assignment

As you are the new chief information officer for the district, the superintendent has asked you to find a solution to this issue. He wants you to determine what type of access students, teachers, ESP staff, and administrators should have at the desktop. In addition, he would like you to draft a set of procedures to enforce that access. For instance, how will the access be monitored? What consequences will staff face for downloading copies of software? etc.

---

[2] A legacy system is one that pre-dates the present systems, but has been retained to provide a specific function such as maintaining an old program specifically to print theater tickets as the new system does not have the functionality.

Potential Resources

Ackerman, R.K. (2002). Desktop security system hides data from interlopers. *Signal*, 57 (2), 68.

Apicella, M. (2003). Hardware safety net. *InfoWorld*, March 10.

Yasin, R. (2000). Telecommuters on security alert: Specialized firewalls, intrusion systems fortify always-on connections, *InternetWeek*, 812, 43.

Adhaero Direct Desktop Security Solutions. (2003). Available at http://www.adhaeroutilities.com.

Desktop Security Access from Checkpoint. (2003). Available at http://www.checkpoint.com.

Horizon Data Systems. (2003). Available at http://www.horizondatasys.com.

Knowledge Storm Security Systems. (2003). Available at http://www.knowledgestorm.com.

Also see the Web sites of various security products such as FoolProof, Fortress, OnGuard, etc. Also see copyright resources under Warlick's Videos.

To See or Not to See

The Background

You are the CIO of the Guildford City Schools. You have about 3,500 computers in 18 schools. The district is trying to move forward with the use of technology and the infrastructure to do so is in place. However, the majority of teachers are woefully unprepared to use technology in their classrooms. A strong technology staff development program has been put into place and progress is being made. However, this is a slow process and will take a couple of years for real change to occur. Your new network manager, Gary Raidner, comes into your office and shuts the door behind him. He is very frustrated with the director of staff development, Mark Wellington. Gary has determined that in response to general teacher concerns that his staff are rifling through their network files he wishes to tightly restrict access to network files. He hopes to restrict access to all staff files; to only those people involved in network administration. That would remove all access to primary repair staff and the staff development staff. Mark, reports Gary, "freaked out" when he told him. Gary is in your office to ensure he has your support.

About a half hour after Gary leaves your office, Mark appears and he is quite perturbed. He articulates his arguments as to why his staff should continue to have access to all files on the network.

Gary Raidner's arguments:

- *Teachers, and other staff, already feel that the IT staff is snooping through everyone's files. So to counteract that opinion, access to files should be restricted.*

- *He feels uncomfortable leaving evaluations, etc. on his own network drive since his staff has access to those files.*

- *Staff should have a basic expectation of privacy for their folders and files.*

Mark Wellington's arguments:

- *The staff development staff members need to be able to access everyone's folders so that when teachers have problems, they can help.*

- *Teachers do not have time to log out and have others log in to assist them with files, etc. That has a negative impact on the ability of staff developers to have a positive affect on instruction.*

- *The move to restrict folder access sends the message to the staff developers that the network staff does not trust them.*

- *Since the network files are not truly private anyway, this adds to the illusion that they are and could cause more problems with staff concerns about being monitored.*

The Assignment

Write a memo disseminating your decision to your two managers. Articulate what factors you considered and who else you may have consulted in making the decision.

A New Car for the Information Superhighway

The Background

You are the technology coordinator for a 1,400 student high school. The school is rich in technology. Each teacher desk and classroom has a computer and many classrooms have small pods of computers. The community is a mixture of working class and white-collar families. Nearly a third of the families are single income households with stay at home mothers.

The Assignment

The school also has a monthly parent meeting. The principal has asked you to prepare a seminar for the next parent's association meeting. He wants you to explain to the parents how to make an informed home computer purchase. He wants you to include the following in the presentation:

- *How to determine your needs*
- *How to read and compare the type of computer advertisements that appear in the newspaper*
- *What are the basic functional statistics of a computer, RAM, HD size, monitor size, etc.*
- *How to choose an Internet service provider*
- *How to choose a printer*

He wants you to put the materials into a PowerPoint or similar presentation. He wants to review it at least two days prior to the meeting.

Potential Resources

Bartholomew (IN) Consolidated School Corporation (2001). Instructional technology update: Guidelines for purchasing a home computer. Available at http://www.bcsc.k12.in.us/docstechnews/tu0111.htm.

CNET. (2003). What to look for in desktops. Available at http://reviews.cnet.com/4520-3118_7-5021315-1.html?legacy=cnet.

Hastings and Prince Edward District School Board. (2003). Suggested home computer purchase specs. Available at http://hpedsb.on.ca/ec/its/homespec.htm.

Internet Public Library. (2003). Pathefinder: Purchasing a home computer. Available at http://www.ipl.org.ar/ref/QUE/PF/buycomputer.html.

Paideia School. (2003). Suggestions for purchasing a home computer. Available at http://www.paideiaschool.org/tech/purchasing.htm.

Sayerville (NJ) Public Schools. (2003). Technology. Available at http://www.sayrevillek12.net/technology.htm.

Also search the Internet to review retail and wholesale computer sales sites.

Passwords or Spot123

The Background

You are the technology coordinator for a large high school of approximately 2,300 students. The school is a fairly typical comprehensive high school. It offers over 100 different courses as diverse as auto shop and Latin. The staff includes approximately 240 teachers and 120 support staff including the maintenance team. The school was an early adopter of technology and staff have had computers on their desks for more than ten years. Generally, the teachers are excellent users of technology within their classrooms. However, they are also less than fastidious about following the policies and procedures articulated by the district IT office. In the past, that has not been a problem, since the assistant superintendent for technology previously held your job and knew that the teachers were generally his biggest supporters. So, when you had problems enforcing some of the district's more routine policies on downloading software or not taking computers home during the summer, she was willing to overlook your teachers' dalliances regarding policy.

However, she retired and you now have a new assistant superintendent for technology. He is very direct and feels that one of his directives from the superintendent is to enforce the district's policies regarding technology. One of those policies is that passwords are to be changed regularly. In fact, he interprets that as changing them at least once every 30 days. Since your school was the first to get individual staff computers, the policy had not been in place when your staff first received machines. So, the previous assistant superintendent had overlooked the policy as it affected your staff. Now, your new assistant superintendent is fairly livid that you have not enforced the password change policy. In fact, you had allowed the utility that would have required the monthly password change to remain disabled. Complicating the situation is that your high school's long serving principal retired last year as well and your new principal wants to show her desire to follow district policies.

Further complicating the situation is that a student teacher's account had been compromised in another school in the district and the student involved hacked into a commercial Web site and caused a great deal of damage. The superintendent is now very concerned about computer security and passwords when a year ago it wasn't on his radar screen at all. Many of your staff members have probably been using the same password for nearly ten years. Some also use the same password for each system and many are on Post It notes left under their keyboards.

You also know many of your teachers will find the need to change passwords as an administrative hassle with no real purpose. They will be difficult and many may simply refuse to change their passwords. If the passwords expire, they will just not use the computers for attendance, etc.

The Assignment

The assistant superintendent for technology has directed you to determine a method of implementing regular change in passwords. Your principal agrees that this issue could be contentious for the staff. So she has asked you to draw up a one-page summary of why there is a need to rotate passwords. Include some suggestions for how to create good passwords.

Potential Resources

Basic password security guidelines. Available at http://www.cse.ucsd.edu/groups/crypto/group/SimplePasswordSecurity.html.

Blacharski, D. (2000). Create order with a strong security policy, *Network Magazine*, July 1, 62.

Clark, E. (2003). Making peace with passwords, *Network Magazine*, October 1, 42.

Generating effective network passwords. Available at http://www.dummies.com/WileyCDA/DummiesArticle/id-250.html.

Password security: Part 1: Are passwords really secure?. Available at http://netsecurity.about.com/library/weekly/aa021703a.htm.

Password security: Part 2: Sometimes less is more. Available at http://netsecurity.about.com/library/weekly/aa021703b.htm.

Also search the Internet using the search terms "basic password security and tips".

Needful Things in the Athletics Office

Description of the District

You are the technology coordinator for Gable High School. Gable High School is a large high school of approximately 1,600 students. There are two other high schools in the district. Both are approximately the same in enrollment. The school has approximately 850 computers and is well networked. The district has recently gone through a migration to a new administrative software package, EagleSchool. Although generally successful, the need to change "the way we have always done it" has caused a fair amount of resistance. The majority of the administration has worked well with you; however, the athletic director has been hard to work with. It has been difficult for him to move off of the legacy system, which he is still using. As part of the "good old boy network" in the district, the previous district Management Information Services (MIS) Director had worked to build a number of specific programming modifications in the legacy system for your athletic director. The previous MIS director and the athletic director had been baseball coaches together earlier in their careers. The previous MIS director retired several years ago, but is still an influence among most of the administrators who are close to retirement themselves. The new MIS director is very frustrated with the situation. She has been trying to move the Gable athletic department onto EagleSchool and has been having no luck. Since the Gable athletic director is not using EagleSchool, the district MIS director is unable to provide the superintendent and the board members with statistics and other data regarding athletic program participation. Recently, the athletic director wrote a long memo to the MIS director and copied you, your principal, and the superintendent. He demands that all efforts to move him to the "new and improved software" be stopped and that "we get a new computer person who understands the needs of the athletic department."

Your principal asks you to get to the bottom of the issue and write up a set of recommendations.

The Background

In doing a little digging, you come up with the following information:

- *The EagleSchool software athletic module is the weakest of the modules of the system. However, since the other high school athletic departments had only used paper systems in the past, they are willing to use it to move into the computer age. Only the Gable HS athletic department ever used the "old system" they are currently trying to retain. The main complaint is that the EagleSchool software limits the amount of characters that can be entered into the notes field for a given student and the athletic trainers do not have enough room to enter their full treatment procedures in a single record for a student. In addition, the system does not allow for word wrap and the trainer has to manually choose a new line every 80 characters. All of the necessary information can be kept in EagleSchool.*

- *EagleSchool does not customize software for individual districts and is unwilling to make any timely changes to the athletics module.*

- *The legacy system is the only system being maintained on the district's old AS/400. The MIS director wants to sell that computer in the next couple of months. All other systems have been moved to newer RS6000 systems. The cost to maintain the AS/400 is approximately $35,000 per year.*

- *The MIS director strongly wants to bring every system in the district into the EagleSchool umbrella so that reporting and maintenance is streamlined.*

- *The previous MIS director is willing to come in and write a new athletic program for his old buddy, but the new MIS director is against him doing so. The cost would be about $10,000 but it would run on the newer RS6000 computers.*

Currently, one of the district MIS staffers has to query the data out of EagleSchool every day and port it into the old athletic system.

The MIS director has been in the district four years. She has had a difficult time dealing with the need to move to EagleSchool. In addition, she is the most senior female in the district and has met a great deal of resistance. She is technically very competent and has supported you on a number of issues since you moved up from a teaching position two years ago.

The athletic director is a true curmudgeon. He is nearly 60 and won't be retiring for a couple more years at least. He doesn't understand technology very well. He is extremely frustrated that the "MIS girl" cannot let him keep his old system. He has let you know he expects you to be loyal to the Gable High School team.

The Assignment

Write a memo to the principal and the superintendent that outlines your suggestions for resolving this issue.

The Vanishing Vendor

Descriptions of the School District and Community

You are the chief information officer for the Prince of Prussia School District that serves approximately 10,000 students in grades K-12. The district operates two high schools, five middle schools, and fifteen elementary schools. All are located within a six square mile area. The district has about 1,350 staff members. Two-thirds of those are faculty members. The district's test scores are regularly among the top ten in the state in all of the areas currently assessed. Over 90% of the students attend a four-year college or university. The district includes approximately 4,000 computers. This number includes approximately 750 Macintoshes, mostly at the elementary level. The district has a robust WAN and each classroom has network and Internet access. Although budgets are always tight, generally, Prince of Prussia has a funding level that allows for the regular replacement of technology equipment and technology is in good repair. E-mail is available for all staff and students and all district communications are sent to the staff using e-mail as the primary medium.

Prince of Prussia serves three suburban communities that are generally bedroom communities within a larger metropolitan area. Parents work outside of the immediate area and often voice concern about having access to teachers or school officials when they need to conference about their children. The population is generally middle class or higher income levels. The community strongly supports education and looks to the schools to be forward thinking.

The Background

You recently found out that the vendor for the administrative software package you use is going out of business. They are being taken over by another vendor who will not be continuing to support the software you currently use. In addition, the new vendor's product is only a student records package and does not include the finance or payroll modules. Those systems will simply not be supported in the future. None of the other districts in your area use the same administrative package. You will now have to quickly choose a new software package and work to implement it. Currently, you have software modules for the following areas:

- *Finance and payroll*
- *Food services*
- *Health services*
- *Human resources*
- *Library circulation and catalog*
- *Student records and scheduling*
- *Student discipline records*
- *Transportation*

Currently you have two MIS staff members. Both know the current systems fairly well, and everything being equal, they will each retire from your district in a couple of years. They have made minor modifications to the original system modules. However, sometimes, their coding has had unintended consequences. They have voiced their opinion that they can easily maintain the current system indefinitely.

When you mention to the rest of the administrative team that the current vendor is going out of business, the business manager is upset about the possible costs of a new system and the migration of the current data. The principals are excited about the chance to obtain better software that provides more data analysis opportunities for them. They also ask you to make sure that the new package includes a parent-accessible grade book. They feel that the parents would really like that type of access to their students' progress. The personnel director would like to see a "more robust" human resources module in the new product. The curriculum director would want to ensure that the new system would allow for "information mining." She had heard at a conference, that such information would be important with the new federal legislation. Later, you speak to the library media coordinator who does not want to migrate to a new system. He likes the current system and would hope that you can continue to maintain it. Similarly, a high school dean calls you to express shock that you want to move to a new discipline system when the current system works so well.

In briefly reviewing your options, you speak to a number of your counterparts in other area districts. Most agree that only two companies provide systems that can provide all of the modules you currently use; SchoolCo and Innovative School Information. Neither of those vendors is inexpensive or perfect. A couple of your colleagues suggest that they started using a number of smaller vendors each providing specialized software modules. One comments that she simply plans to maintain the software on her own and save some money in not having to pay for yearly technical support. She feels that with the way budgets have been going lately, this is a good option for her district. One of your colleagues gives you a list of questions his district asked when they migrated to a new system because of y2k (See Figure 2.3). He felt it might be helpful.

The Assignment

After speaking to everyone, you are more confused and concerned than before. You then speak to the associate superintendent who tells you that she and the superintendent are concerned about the news of the need to find a system. They would like a detailed memo that they can share with the Board of Education explaining the process you will use to determine the requirements of the new system and a timeline outlining the key dates and milestones in the process. She reminds you that today is already September 1 and that the project will have to be included in tentative budget allocations that the Board will receive the following April.

She further reminds you that you will need to include who should be involved in making a recommendation to the Board of Education. In addition, you will need to articulate the general concerns you might have about needing to migrate from your current system. You will also need to articulate the various options available from which you will recommend. Provide the general advantages and disadvantages of each of those options. If possible, include your first impressions of which direction you are leaning and why.

The Two "Other" Systems

The two systems that your colleagues have helped you to identify each have some significant strengths and weaknesses. Although, there are other commercial options, none of them are as viable as these. If you decide to go with a commercial product, your choice would be one of these two systems.

Figure 2.1 SchoolCO Software System

Strengths	Weaknesses
Client software works on both platforms	All state reports not included
Simple user interface	No local user group
Allows for parent access to view gradebooks	Medical records module very weak
Initial training and set up would be minimal	Requires use of proprietary gradebook program
Less expensive than other options	Does not support library catalog

---

Figure 2.2 Innovative School Information

Strengths	Weaknesses
Excellent data array strategies	Steep learning curve to use effectively
Easy to export data	Does not work support Macintosh use
Much of the data is table verified	Does not support library catalog
Strong state level user group	Most expensive option
Allows for remote access of grades and attendance via the web	
Special education IEP generator available	

Figure 2.3: Administrative Software Questions

Dear Tech. Coordinator,
We asked these questions of both the vendor salespeople and of the other districts where we did site visits. They helped us gather the right information. Hopefully they will help you.

Steve Slade,
Asst. Supt. for Technology

What software do you currently use?
- On what platform/hardware configuration can the system run?
- How many users can be supported?
- Does it support both Macs & PCs? (if applicable)
- What are the annual maintenance costs?
- Do you receive the source code as part of the purchase?

Are users happy with the level of support received?
- Who is the primary software contact?

What constitutes the initial training provided?

Is training offered locally by the vendor?

Is there a state level users' group?
- If yes, how often do they meet?

Is there a local or regional users' group?
- If yes, how often do they meet?

Are all/most state board of education reports part of the software package?
- If yes, which ones if any are not covered?
- If no, which reports are covered?
- Any serious problems in state reporting?

How often is the software updated?
- Are there additional fees for updates?

What kind of data conversion support can you offer?

How easy is it to extract data to a .csv or similar format?

Does the software package a standard report writer (Crystal Reports, Cognos Impromptu)?
- If yes, which one?

How many people are realistically necessary to support the system?

How reliable is the system?

What do users like the most about the system?

What are the system's drawbacks?

Who could we talk to for more in-depth information?

Can you provide school references?

Potential Resources

Capterra – The enterprise software center. (2003). Available at http://www.capterra.com/find. This site leads one through a list of questions to ask to different staff members in the organization. Although, it is focused on business, it can be adapted to education.

Farnsworth, C. (2002). Data collection and use in schools. Honolulu, HI: Pacific Resources for Education and Learning. ERIC number: ED467664.

Smith, R., Nansen, C. & Shouten, J. F. (1998). Programs that manage: A look at the giants in school-management software. Electronic School. March. Available at http://www.electronic-school.com/0398f9.html.

Threet, S. (2001). Administrative software: increasing accountability. Media & Methods. 37 (5), 32-33.

Vecchioli, Lisa (1999). A process for evaluating student records management software. Practical Assessment, Research & Evaluation, 6(14).

Chapter 3

Managing People

A Favor for the Boss

The Background

You receive a phone call from your superintendent telling you to expect a call from a friend of hers who is the superintendent of the Sundale School District. The other superintendent calls within the hour. He is looking to hire a new technology director and your boss offered your help. Since the previous technology director left the state, he is uncomfortable conducting the interviews without someone with technical knowledge. He is hoping you can put together a list of questions that his non-technical administrators can ask and then identify some areas that you could cover in a technical interview with the finalists. He ends by saying that he will send you some basic information about the district.

Description of the School District and Community

The Sundale Community School District is small, serving 1,200 K-12 students in three buildings located near your own district. The secondary school serves grades 7-12 with about 600 students. The two elementary schools each serve about 300 students. The schools are each connected to the Internet and have basic LANs but they have no WAN infrastructure. The district has about 200 computers in the secondary school and about 75 in each elementary school. There is a mixture of PCs and Macs in each building. The district has a decent funding structure for technology, but it needs a better overall plan about how to provide for continuing support of technology. The district is standardized on using MS Office at the secondary school and AppleWorks at the elementary schools.

The staff development program has been nothing more than your basic smorgasbord approach. About 35% of the teachers are active technology users with a higher percentage at the elementary level. The district has a typical administrative software program and the elementary schools use phone lines to connect to the secondary school where the MIS systems are located. The district Web site is in sad shape and some sections have not been updated in more than a year. There are three technical staff in the district: an MIS systems staffer, a network administrator, and a repair technician.

The Assignment

Write a letter to Sundale's superintendent, outlining the questions he should include in his interviews. For each question, provide sample or expected answers and a rationale as to why those questions should be included. Secondly, enumerate the issues you would be covering in a technical interview with a finalist. Ensure that you cover the following areas within the set of sample questions you develop for the administrators to ask:

- *Educational philosophy and pedagogy*
- *Educational technology philosophy*
- *Educational technology integration*
- *General administrative questions*
- *Hardware, software, and networking experience*
- *Information and technology literacy education*
- *Supervision and management of technical staff*
- *Technology staff development*
- *Vision of future developments in technology*

For the technical portion of the interview, outline what areas you will cover with the finalist and why each of those areas is important. One of your colleagues also sends you a listing of questions he used when hiring.

Exhibit 1:
Instructional Technology Department Chair Interview Questions

- *In your experience, what does a successful staff development program in technology look like?*
- *Stepping into a successful program, what do you see your role being?*
- *If you are being asked to introduce a school-wide technology change (attendance/grades online, time cards, etc.) what do you view as the steps necessary to make it a success?*

- *What does a technology-enriched classroom like? Now and in the future (5 years).*

- *What role should technology play in the lives of high school students?*

- *What innovative strategies have you seen employed for integrating technology into the classroom?*

- *What experience have you had in teaching adults?*

- *How is teaching adults different from teaching younger students?*

- *What is the main responsibility or challenge of lab supervisors?*

- *How would you work to increase the feeling of connection between the Northfield lab supervisors and the Winnetka lab supervisors?*

- *What is the last book that you read?*

- *How would you define your leadership style?*

- *What are your software skills? Speak to your most significant strengths and weaknesses.*

Potential Resources

Hobsons College View. (2003). *Top job interview questions.* Available at http://www.collegeview.com/career/interviewing/top_questions/questions.html.

Kosmoski, G. J. (1999). *How to land the best jobs in school administration: The self-help workbook for practicing and aspiring school administrators.* Thousand Oaks, CA: Corwin Press.

Litvin, J. S. (2003). *Tough interview questions and the answers managers want.* Available at http://www.microsearchsf.com/intrvucw.htm.

MSN Careers. (2003). *Illegal questions.* Available at http://editorial.careers.msn.com/articles/illegal/.

Murray, J. P. (1999). Interviewing to hire competent community college faculty, *Community College Review, 27(1),* 41-56.

University of South Carolina. (2003). *Frequently asked interview questions.* Available at http://www.libsci.sc.edu/career/invufaqs.htm.

Motivating and Retaining Technical Staff

Description of the School District and Community

Woodlawn Community School District is a moderate sized district with approximately 2,500 students in six school buildings. It is just outside a major urban center and the schools cover three smaller towns. The district employs 243 staff members of all types, including eight IT staff members. The district has a wide area network and each building is networked. The MIS systems that are in place are functional and tied together for data sharing. Each school has computers in most classrooms, but some of the computers are more than five years old. Each school has a centralized software inventory, but teachers also bring in their own programs from home. The district is growing, as the smaller towns are becoming de facto suburbs. Industry and commerce in the communities served by the district are generally limited to those of an agricultural nature. However, the district is growing in a very controlled way due to the forethought of the local community planners, and taxes and assessments are keeping up with student enrollment, at least for now.

Woodlawn Community School District has come under new leadership. Dr. Hazel Timmons has been brought in to prepare the district for the future. The school board feels that there are a number of areas in which the district is lagging behind. You are the newly hired technology director and have been asked to create a more professional and service-oriented IT department than has been available to support the district in the past.

The Background

Most of the IT staff hired in the past were parents or teacher-aides who liked computers or wanted the higher wages available in the IT jobs. Only one of the IT staff members has not been trained on the job and that is the MIS manager. She has been in the district since 1979. All of the other members of the IT department have less than five years in the district and only one has been in the IT department for more than 18 months. In the past, as soon as the district put the resources into an IT staff member to get them trained in computer repair or networking, they moved to a higher paying corporate job.

Due to the general lack of experience and formal training, the IT department has not been well orchestrated in the past. As soon as the department would start to work well together, personnel changes would require that the process start anew. The district is nearly without procedures or policies regarding the day-to-day management of technology except for the MIS systems.

The Assignment

Dr. Timmons has asked that you develop a plan to create a more motivated and professional IT department. She would like you to review what types of professional development and training opportunities that they have. She wants to know how to attract and retain high quality IT staff that will stay in the district. At present you have two openings among the eight positions in the district. Both are computer repair positions. However, both previous staff members were also doing some network administration as well. Dr. Timmons has offered you to increase the starting wage by up to 20 percent if you can find stronger candidates who will be more permanent as well.

She wants you to review the job descriptions for the vacant positions and revise them to require prior technology experience and/or formal training. She also wants you to develop a professional development program for your staff for her review prior to the next Board Meeting. She is willing to provide you with up to $20,000 for the professional development of your staff, if you can provide an excellent plan and articulate how you will assess its success. Dr. Timmons also suggests that you review the staff development program criteria set up by the National Staff Development Council. She feels they do really great work.

Figure 3.1 The IT Department

Staff Member	Job Title	Degree/Certification	Location	Years in Position
Karen Anderson	MIS Manager	B.S. Computer science, 1978	Central office	19
Janet Green	Data processing operator	B.A. Home economics, 1984	Central office	2
Rod Tchishfrie	Network manager	Novell C.N.A. 6.x A+ certified	East School	1
Ken Powers	Asst. Net. Manager	A+ certified	Southeast Jr. H.S.	2
Vacant	Computer repair specialist		West School	
Ted Meyers	Computer repair specialist	B.Ed. Physical Education, 2000 Novell C.N.A. 6.x	South School	1
Otar Hammadi	Computer repair/Web design	None	Northwest Jr. H.S.	1
Vacant	Computer repair specialist/clerk		East School	2

Chapter Three: Managing People

Below is the job description for the two vacant positions as they stand. They appear to need some updating.

Figure 3.2 Computer Repair Specialist Job Description

Woodlawn Schools

Job Description

JOB TITLE: Computer Repair Specialist   **LOCATION:** West
DEPARTMENT: IT   **SUPERVISED BY:** Networking Manager
HOURS: 8/Day   **GRADE:** T-1

POSITION SUMMARY:
The position is responsible for technology support activities that include diagnosis of problems, initial attempts to fix the problem, and referrals to repair agencies. In addition, this person sets up hardware, software, and network communications within the building and is among the first to whom district employees (teachers and others) turn with technology-related problems and inquiries.

QUALIFICATIONS - EXPERIENCE - KNOWLEDGE:
- *Two- or four-year college degree, and/or -*
- *Three or more years experience working with computer hardware/software and networking*
- *Highly proficient with WIN95, Apple OS, Novell and network support*
- *Competent in computer and peripheral hardware troubleshooting and maintenance*
- *Knowledgeable in office software (i.e. word processor, spreadsheet, database, e-mail, etc.)*

ESSENTIAL DUTIES
- *Provide site support to users (including training for administrative staff), as well as support for equipment and LAN (daily operations, maintenance and repair)*
- *Computer set-up and inventory, software installation, and network configuration*
- *Network maintenance and support for 400+ nodes and Novell 4.11 servers on an Ethernet LAN*
- *Hardware maintenance with some minor repairs done in house*
- *NOTE: There are no teaching or classroom duties associated with this job*

SKILLS REQUIRED
- Ability to interact positively and effectively with all staff
- Ability to communicate clearly and establish an effective working relationship with users and coworkers
- Willingness to perform duties in accordance with Board of Education policies and District requirements
- Capacity to interpret technical manuals and follow procedures
- Ability to set up, operate, maintain and repair personal computers, peripherals and systems
- Knowledgeable in popular software packages (i.e. Work, Excel, Access, Print Shop, etc)
- Advanced knowledge of Windows 95 as well as working knowledge of Novell OS and networking principles (i.e. Ethernet, IPX, TCP/IP, etc.)
- Ability to perform hardware and software upgrades/configurations on servers and end nodes
- Able to create network user profiles, environments and settings to accommodate access to network resources
- Well organized and able to work under limited supervision (required to carry pager)
- Willingness to remain well informed on computer technology and software developments through formal and informal methods

PHYSICAL DEMANDS:
While performing the duties of this job, the employee is regularly required to sit and talk or hear; stand; walk; operate a computer and reach with hands and arms and will frequently repeat the same hand, arm, or finger motion such as typing. Specific vision abilities required by this job include close vision at a video display terminal or monitor. The employee may occasionally lift up to 75 pounds such as boxes of paper, microcomputer, printers, and scanners.

WORK ENVIRONMENT:
The noise level in the work environment is usually moderate. The employee frequently must meet multiple demands from several people.

Potential Resources

Hayes, K. (2001). School librarians as staff developers, Book Report, 19(4), 6-8.

LeTendre, B.G..(2000). 6 Steps to a solution, Journal of Staff Development; 21(1), 20-25.

Murphy, M. (2002). Let's change staff development to professional learning, Principal, 81(4),16-17.

National Staff Development Council. (2003).

Phillips, J. L. & Phillips, P. P. (2002). Reasons why training and development fails...and what you can do about it, Training, 39(9), 78-82+.

Sorge, D. H.& Russell, J. D. (2000). A strategy for effective change in instructional behavior: Staff development that works, Educational Technology, 40(6), 46-48.

Additional Questions

Some districts use IT recruiters or search firms to hire higher level IT staff in the same way that most school boards use a search firm to hire superintendents or other executive positions. What are the advantages and disadvantages of using professional recruiters to assist in the placement of IT staff within a district?

Some districts offer signing bonuses to new employees who agree to stay with the district for a given amount of time. What might be the advantages to doing so for IT staff within the district? The disadvantages? What if you expanded signing bonuses to hard to find teaching positions such as chemistry teachers, special educators, or school library media specialists?

Skills or Else!

Descriptions of the School District and Community

Loess Hills Consolidated Schools is in the southwestern corner of a Midwestern state. The district serves three small communities and the surrounding farmlands. It is generally a rural district including five elementary schools, a middle school and a high school. The district employs approximately 650 staff members of all types. The teaching staff averages 14.2 years of teaching experience. Forty-two percent of the teachers hold masters degrees. Most of the teachers have computers at home. Only about half of the support staff have computers at home. All staff members are under a collective bargaining agreement. The district has invested a great deal into creating a strong technology program focusing on preparing children for the future world of work. A recent bond issue included significant funding for technology. Each classroom has at least one computer and all computers in the district are networked to the Internet.

The area is largely agricultural and the economy in the area has not flourished for the past ten years. The largest single private employer in the area, HealthOne, is a firm that supports health care software. The jobs at HealthOne are highly sought after. However, due to the technical nature of the positions, many area residents have had to go back to the local community college to learn the skills necessary to apply for these newer jobs. Unfortunately, they are still not as well paying as those previously available at the meat packing plant that closed ten years ago.

The Background

Recently a number of vocal critics in the community have begun to decry the funding of technology because their children have said their teachers never use the computers. Although students do use computers in some classes, most teachers do not truly integrate them into instruction. An administrator caught off guard on the issue was partially quoted as saying, "Well, the older teachers don't want to use the computers and we can't force them." This has caused a great deal of angst and turmoil among the administration and the Board of Education.

In reality, there is some reason for the community to be concerned. The superintendent asked you to meet with her about the issue. She agrees with you that only two of the elementary schools really use computers effectively within their curriculum. You both agree that the middle school does an excellent job integrating technology mostly due to the fact that the middle school principal and assistant principal are both strong supporters of technology and have made technology skills a litmus test for newer hires. However, the superintendent is concerned that the high school teachers and some of the elementary teachers have not stepped up to the plate regarding technology integration. In fact, the superintendent does not use e-mail for district communications because so few of the high school teachers check their e-mail regularly. A number of administrators are also less than fully supportive of technology. The superintendent also shares with you that a number of the other area school districts have implemented mandatory technology skills for teachers. However, the success of those programs has varied greatly. In general, the technology skills required by these districts are extremely minimal and have included such basic skills as "be able to send a voice mail message" and "open a new document in a word processor."

The Assignment

The superintendent tells you that she has received a great deal of pressure from the school board to solve the problem. She has decided that the district does need technology skill standards. However, she has not yet determined if they should be requirements or expectations. She wants you to put together a recommendation to be presented to the Board as to whether or not to propose required technology skills for all staff as part of the upcoming contract negotiations. She gives you the following questions that need to be answered in your recommendation:

- *Do you believe that the district should implement technology skills standards for teachers? Support staff?*

- *If so, what should those basic skills be based upon? Should they be clearly articulated to specific software or should they be more general abstractions? (Should they align with national standards such as ISTE's standards for teachers?)*

- *Who will assess these skills? (How will they be assessed?)*

- *If you recommend not requiring skills, what incentives can be given to teachers without increasing the budget?*

- *If you recommend required skills, what consequences, if any, will happen to those staff that do not fulfill the requirements?*

- *Should the skills be phased in? If so, how long should the staff be given?*

- *What support would you need to implement your recommendations?*

- *Will training be provided? If so, who will deliver this and how?*

- *How should the Board and superintendent present your recommendations to the community? To the staff?*

Potential Resources

ISTE's National Educational Technology Standards for Teachers (NETS) available at http://www.iste.org/standards/.

Illinois Technology Standards available at http://talent.ed.uiuc.edu/docs/IllinoisStateTechnologyStandards.pdf.

NCREL Critical Issue: Providing Professional Development for Effective Technology Use available at http://www.ncrel.org/sdrs/areas/issues/methods/technlgy/te1000.htm

Technology Skills and Implementation for Teachers available at http://profiler.scrtec.org/smfl/survey.jsp?survey_id=1354.

Bennett, L. (2001). Technology standards for the preparation of teachers, International Journal of Social Education, 15(2) 1-11.

Bradshaw, L. K. (2002). Technology for teaching and learning: Strategies for staff development and follow-up support, Journal of Technology and Teacher Education, 10 (1), 131-50.

Brush, T. ed. (2003). Introduction to the special issue on preparing tomorrow's teachers to use technology, Educational Technology Research and Development, 51(1), 39-40.

Burns, M. (2002). From black and white to color: Technology, professional development and changing practice, T.H.E. Journal, June.

Dugger, W. E. (2002). Standards for technological literacy, Tech Directions, 61(8) 27-31.

Krueger, K., Hansen, L., Smaldino, S. E. (200) Preservice teacher technology competencies, TechTrends, 44 (3), 47-50.

Johnson, Doug. The Indispensable Teacher's Guide to Computer Skills, 2nd edition. Worthington, OH: Linworth Publishing.

Passig, D. (2001). Future online teachers' scaffolding: what kind of advanced technological innovations would teachers like to see in future distance training projects? Journal of Technology and Teacher Education, 9 (4) 599-605.

Sandholtz, J. H. (2001). Learning to teach with technology: a comparison of teacher development programs, Journal of Technology and Teacher Education, 9(3) 349+.

The Managers' Ultimatum

Description of the District

You are the director of technology for a moderate sized suburban high school district. The district is comprised of five traditional high schools, an alternative center, and an administrative and professional development center. Each of the high schools has an enrollment of approximately 2,100 students. Three of the district's schools perform above state averages. The other two are approximately average with regard to student performance.

The district is networked via a redundant fiber wide area network (WAN). All of the buildings are strongly positioned with regard to computer technology. The district's telephone system is relatively new and fully functional. The technology staff development program is excellent and has been recognized by the state as a model program. The district's administrative software packages were installed in the past two years, and the MIS staff is still working to totally convert the district to the new system.

The Background

Your IT department is structured around five sub-departments; the help desk managed by the network manager and her assistant, MIS services led by a systems analyst, the telephone systems manager, the instructional technology department headed by the instructional technology department chair, and the library and audio-visual department headed by a department chair. The seventh manager is the technology staff development manager. All are high performing staff members, but each one has strengths and weaknesses. Together they supervise approximately 75 staff members across all seven buildings. At the end of the previous school year, you brought in a team-building consultant to assist the managers in interacting with each other. Overall, the managers do a good job, but they are constantly fighting over who is responsible for what.

The network manager's previous evaluation showed some need for improvement in her interpersonal skills, but technically she is excellent. The other managers all received good evaluations, but complained about one or more of the peers during and after their evaluations. Only the instructional technology chair received an excellent evaluation.

Several of your managers asked to meet with you. They present you with a petition demanding that you fire the network manager. The telephone systems manager, the library department chair, the systems analyst, the assistant network manager, and the staff development manager all signed the petition. They have said they will resign if you do not fire her. They also tell you they discussed the issue with the instructional technology chair, but he decided not to sign.

You told them you would get back to them in a few days. You go back to your office and call the instructional technology chair. He tells you he feels the issue is personality related. He also feels that it isn't his place to tell you how to deal with your other managers. He also feels they are ganging up on her. You all know that she did not have any real management experience when she was hired 18 months ago, but she was the best choice at the time. Your secretary tells you not to trust the assistant network manager who she feels is probably the ringleader and looking for a promotion. The wide area network administrator, who also works for the network manager says the network manager is fine, but she and her assistant just have very different personalities.

The network manager is very sensitive but does tend to be overbearing and occasionally just plain rude. She does mean well and has always tried to improve when you have sat down to give her constructive criticism. She does not like her assistant and does not trust him. She also fights constantly with the systems analyst. They were nearly best friends and then the assistant manager appears to have come between them. You did have to give her a written reprimand for swearing at an employee in front of a salesperson.

The Assignment

In speaking with the assistant superintendent for human resources, she outlines a couple of options. You could reassign the network manager to the role of the WAN administrator and promote the assistant manager to manager and the WAN administrator to the assistant manager position. You could fire the manager outright, but you don't think you can do that without a remediation period. You could ignore the petition entirely. Decide how you want to proceed and articulate the pros and cons in writing so you can discuss them with the superintendent and the assistant superintendent for human resources.

Additional Information

Figure 3.3 Network Manager's Last Annual Evaluation

Township High School District R14

May 14, 2004

TO: Superintendent
FROM: Director of Technology
RE: Lindsay Gordan's Annual Evaluation

Lindsay Gordan has done much excellent work over the course of the past year. The primary objectives that Lindsay accomplished include:

- *Planning for the network infrastructure at Ridgefield and overseeing its implementation. This has gone particularly well. Lindsay has worked hard in this endeavor as well as committing a great deal of time to orchestrating the move.*

- *The migration to GroupWise for the staff. This project went exceedingly well. Lindsay worked very well with Dan Gomez and Dave Evans in orchestrating this fairly intense project.*

- *Revitalization of the network. Lindsay has done an excellent job in putting a plan in place to reorganize and improve the network infrastructure. The segmentation of the network will greatly improve performance. In addition, Lindsay has instituted DHCP addressing for the network, which makes maintaining IP addresses much easier.*

- *Reorganization of WAN data services. Lindsay worked tirelessly to ensure that service interruptions did not occur and that we would rely on the infrastructure to be more efficient for the needs of the individual schools. More work has been accomplished in the last 12 months regarding data services than in the previous 4 years of operations and costs have gone down. This has included the migration to ICN from Beria and less reliance on consultants.*

Lindsey has also been involved in a large number of smaller projects that have also generally gone very well. Her technical skills are excellent. Lindsay and I agree that we need to continue to improve her management skills. We have also talked about her need to control her emotions with regard to end users or vendors from time to time.

Overall, I believe Lindsay is an excellent addition to the district family and that she has a great deal more potential as well.

Potential Resources

Generally, resources in this area will need to come through your human resources department or law firm. Employee discipline and corrective action issues are also often included within each state's school code. Some general information may be obtained from the following sources.

> BLR. (2003). *Human resources answers now.* Available at http://www1.hrnext.com/index.cfm?source=MiQ&effort=318.
>
> Encina, G.B. (2003). *Firing with dignity.* Available at http://www.cnr.berkeley.edu/ucce50/ag-labor/7article/article19.htm.
>
> Hafner, A. W.& Kibble-Smith, B. G.(1988). Managerial responsibility for employee discipline, *Library Journal, 113*(8), 41-44.
>
> McNamara, C. (2003). *The basics of firing an employee.* Available at http://www.mapnp.org/library/emp_perf/prf_issu/firing/basics.htm.

Additional Questions

What might you do differently, if anything, if Lindsay was a minority, disabled, or over 40 years old?

Depending upon your decision, what will you tell your other managers? Unless you fire Lindsay, they may not know what action(s) you decided to take. Should they be informed?

Chapter 4

Instructional Issues

Computer Course Requirement

Description of the District

You have been hired as a consultant for a medium sized far-suburban high school. It was a nearly rural high school only five years ago and is now in the process of growing quickly due to suburban sprawl. The towns encompassed by the district are generally conservative and the taxes are not keeping up with the growth. All areas of the communities are being stretched to the limit by the growth causing each taxing body to take a critical look at all expenses. The school board is doing its best to improve the district as the student body increases and are making strides to raise the academic bar as well. Some of the staff has been resistant, but many are working hard to improve both instruction and student motivation.

In addition to the high school, the district maintains three middle schools grades 6 to 8 and nine elementary schools K-5. At each of the middle schools, technology instruction is unique. At North Middle School, the principal is a strong supporter of technology and has a strong technology program for all students. At Park Middle School, the technology program is nearly non-existent due to the efforts or lack thereof, of its technology teachers. Their program is haphazard and few students graduate eighth grade with any real technology skills. At Central Middle School, a new principal is supportive of technology, but a lack of physical space due to overcrowding makes it nearly impossible to offer regular technology instruction to its students.

The Background

The School Board added a computer education requirement for high school graduation, but did not articulate how the requirement was to be met. You have been brought in to help the high school determine what to present to the Board regarding how to meet the requirement. There are several groups concerned about this new graduation requirement.

The first group is made up of business education teachers who have campaigned for this requirement so that all students will take the high school computer applications course. This course is strongly based in keyboarding, but does provide for a small amount of word processing and Internet searching. The high school principal does not feel this course is strong enough to really meet the Board's intention.

Another group of teachers led by the high school technology coordinator wishes to see a stronger course that focuses on meeting state and national technology guidelines. However, such a course would have a very negative impact on the business education program, possibly costing the jobs of tenured teachers. A number of younger teachers are willing and able to teach such a new course, but they range in certification from mathematics to art.

The middle school teachers and their administrators are strongly supportive of the requirement being able to be met through either a middle school computer applications course or a proficiency exam for exiting eighth graders. However, past attempts to allow for proficiency tests to skip the high school computer applications has met with contentious failure. The tests have always been heavily weighted on keyboarding and students have done poorly. The middle school teachers have complained that the weighting of keyboarding proficiency has been exaggerated. They feel the keyboarding component should be only a minimal section of the exam and if students could pass the other sections, the keyboarding section should not weigh enough to fail them.

The last group of teachers wishes that all students would take an online course, since they feel that many colleges and universities are beginning to offer online courses in so many cases. Though a small group, these teachers feel that experience in an online learning situation is more important than actual skill with word processing or presentation software. In fact, they advocate that most students already have picked those skills up at home or in elementary and middle school.

The Assignment

You are to articulate in a white paper to the assistant superintendent for curriculum and staff development your recommendations for meeting the new computer graduation requirement. The assistant superintendent also told you that if you think the addition of the requirement was a mistake, you could recommend its repeal.

Additional Information

Below are the courses presently offered at the secondary level that are technology related.

Figure 4.1 High School Computer Courses

Course Title	Department	% of Students Enrolled
Computer applications	Business Education	8%
Computer programming 1	Mathematics	6%
Computer programming 2	Mathematics	2%
Computer graphics	Art	4%

Figure 4.2 Middle School Computer Courses

School	Course	Grade Level
North MS	Computer explorations	6th – required
North MS	Word processing	7th – elective
North MS	Advance computers	8th – elective
Park MS	Keyboarding	6th – required
Park MS	Keyboarding II	7th or 8th – required
Central MS	Keyboarding	6th or 8th – required

Potential Resources

Eisenberg, M.B. (2001). Beyond the bells and whistles: Technology skills for a purpose. MultiMedia Schools, 8 (3), 44-48, 50-51.

Eisenberg, M. B., & Berkowitz, R. E. (2000). Teaching information & technology skills: The Big6 in secondary schools. Worthington, Ohio: Linworth Publishing.

Eisenberg, M. B. & Johnson, D. (2002). Learning and teaching information technology: Computer skills in context. ERIC Digest.

Fulton, K. (1997). Learning in the digital age: Insights into the issues. The skills students need for technological fluency. Santa Monica, CA: Milken Family Foundation. Available at http://www.mff.org/pubs/ME164.pdf.

Houtz, L.E. & Gupta, U.G. (2001). Nebraska High School Students' Computer Skills and Attitudes, Journal of Research on Computing in Education, 33 (3), 316-27.

North Carolina State Board of Education. (2003). Report of 1998-99 Student Performance North Carolina Tests of Computer Skills. Reporting on the Classes of 2001-2003 for the State and 117 Public School Systems and 61 Charter Schools. Raleigh, NC: North Carolina State Dept. of Public Instruction.

Salpeter, J. (2003). 21st century skills: Will our students be prepared. Technology & Learning. 17-26.

Sands, C. (2003). Techie training for students. Technology & Learning, 36-38.

Wagner, J.G. (2001) Getting back to basics, Keying In, 12(1), September.

Absentee Teachers in the Labs and Libraries

Description of the District

You are the district media and technology director of a large urban school district. You serve three high schools, four middle schools, and sixteen elementary schools. In addition, you manage a central processing center for library materials, a technology repair activity, and a technology staff development center. The town and its suburbs encompassed by the district are generally working class communities although some of the suburban areas are fairly affluent. The teachers' union in the district is strong but generally supportive of instructional change if involved in those changes from the start.

The Background

In the past four years, class sizes at the elementary schools have gone up to over 25 students in the average class. Classroom teachers rely on the specials teachers to give them planning time. They are presently released from duties during art, music, physical education, and Spanish classes. However, their classes also go to the library and the computer lab weekly in the primary grades. The teachers are supposed to stay with their students for those instructional periods, but few do. Most of the elementary principals are not prone to support requiring teachers to stay in the computer labs or libraries. They feel that the time is better used by the teachers to plan or grade papers.

A few of the principals including one who was previously a school library media specialist are supportive of moving to a more flexible scheduling solution for the school libraries and the computer labs, but they have asked for your help. They have asked you to research the advantages and disadvantages of moving to flexible scheduling for their schools. They have agreed to make the proposal for the change to the superintendent's cabinet.

The Assignment

The principals were told in speaking with the assistant superintendent for elementary education that a proposal to change would need to be supported by research. They feel this is necessary since the teachers' union will most likely want to keep the time for teacher planning unless there is research to support the changes. They have asked you to prepare an annotated bibliography to support the use of flexible library scheduling in their elementary schools. In addition, they would like to see any research that would support flexible scheduling of the computer labs as well.

Potential Resources

American Association of School Librarians. (2000). Position statement on flexible scheduling available at http://www.ala.org/aasl/positions/ps_flexible.html.

Buchanan. J. (1991). Flexible library media programs. Englewood, CO: Libraries Unlimited.

Everhart, N. (2003). Controversial issues in school librarianship. Worthington, OH: Linworth.

Johnson, D. (2003). Doug Johnson's Web site available at http://www.doug-johnson.com.

Ohlrich, K. B. (1992). Flexible scheduling: The dream vs. reality, School Library Journal, 38 (5), 35-38.

Going to School at Home?

Description of the District

You are the Chief Information Officer for the Kodiak Independent School District. Kodiak is a city of approximately 120,000 people. The school district includes more than 25 schools. The teachers' union is highly organized and occasionally adversarial. The school district is an average urban district. It has the problems of large cities. School achievement is not where the administration would like it to be. The teachers claim that lower class sizes and more dollars for professional development would improve the scores.

The Background

The staff has been asked to participate in additional staff development training. Included in this training was the requirement within the last contract for each teacher to complete two graduate courses. One was to be a special education course and the other was to be a content area course. Because the previous superintendent felt that online courses had little academic rigor, she disallowed any video tele-course or online course from meeting the graduate course requirement. However, that was not well publicized by anyone from the human resources department or the union office. The state university, which had an excellent special education program, was offering a number of online courses in special education. A large number of teachers took the courses, but are now being told that the courses do not meet the specifications due to the fact they were online courses.

Additionally, a small number of teachers did take some video courses from a local private college known for its "pay your fee, get your B" attitude. These teachers are claiming that they should also be allowed to count their video course. The video courses are well known for providing substandard instruction and requiring nearly no effort to pass the courses. However, the private school in question has an above average undergraduate teacher education program and has numerous ties with the district in other areas as well. One of the school board members is also employed by the private school in question and has been very defensive of the school's graduate program in the past.

Compounding the problem is that you are hoping to propose a number of online courses for the high schools for the next academic year. You already anticipate that the teachers' union will not be supportive of the program since they may view it as taking away classroom jobs.

The Assignment

Write a memo to the superintendent and the director of human resources that outlines your suggestions for resolving this issue.

Potential Resources

>Allen, G.D. (2003). *A survey of online mathematics course basics, The College Mathematics Journal, 34(4), 270.*

>Carol, R. (2003). *Home is increasingly where the school is. Milwaukee Journal Sentinel, August 24, 12A.*

>Carr-Chellman, A. & Duchastel, P. (2001). *The ideal online course, Library Trends, 50 (1), 145-161.*

>Loceff, M. (2003). *My day, The Chronicle of Higher Education, 49 (37), A.8.*

>*Maintaining standards in online courses, The Chronicle of Higher Education, 49(22), B.17.*

>Wilson, R. (2001). *Virtual university provides new opportunities for students. Kentucky Monthly, August 1, 16.*

You may also want to review the Web sites of universities with strong online or other distant learning programs.

Block Scheduling in the High Schools

Description of the District

You are the district media and technology director of a large urban school district. You serve three high schools, four middle schools, and sixteen elementary schools. In addition, you manage a central processing center for library materials, a technology repair center, and a technology staff development center. Each high school has approximately 1,000 students. The town and its suburbs encompassed by the district are generally working class communities although some of the suburban areas are fairly affluent. The teachers' union in the district is strong but generally supportive of instructional change if involved in those changes from the start.

The Background

Presently, each of your high school Library Resource Centers (LRCs) is well staffed with two certified library media specialists and four clerical staff members. The clerical staff is made up of an audio-visual (AV) technician, two circulation clerks, and a periodicals clerk/secretary. Each high school also has a dedicated computer repair person and a technology facilitator in addition to the LRC staff.

The assistant superintendent for secondary education has been charged with reviewing all staffing at the high school level in light of the fact the school board has decided to move to a 4 x 4 block schedule at each of the high schools. She is not particularly familiar with your school library program, but has always been supportive of your program and its staffing level. However, the assistant superintendent for finance has been strongly pushing to cut the LRC staff since students will no longer have study halls from which to go to the LRCs. So, your program is somewhat on the defensive.

The Assignment

The assistant superintendent for secondary education has asked you to develop a white paper summarizing the potential impact of the new block scheduling on your LRC and computer programs. In addition to a summary of existing research, she needs to you articulate a plan to prepare your LRC and computer staffs for the transition to block scheduling. Include any changes in staffing and a completely articulated staff development plan for both your staff and the high school teachers as well.

Potential Resources

Atalig, K. (2003) Year-round scheduling in Hawaii's school library media centers, Knowledge Quest, 32(2), 30-34.

Everhart, N. (2003). The impact of year-round schools on the library media program, Knowledge Quest, 32(2), 30-34.

Gierke, C. (1999). What is behind block scheduling? Book Report, 18(2), 18-20.

Shaw, M.K. (1999). Block scheduling and its impact on the school library media center. Westport, CT: Greenwood Press.

Teger, N.L. and Nunn, D. (1999). Impact of block schedules on library media centers, Knowledge Quest, 28(2), 10-11+.

Teger, N. L., Ed. (1996). Block scheduling. Block schedules: a restructuring agenda and block scheduling: impact on library media programs and block scheduling: comments from inside the media center, Florida Media Quarterly, 21(2), 7-10+.

Also search the archives of LM_Net and other school library listservs for previous conversations on this subject.

Typing to Graduate

Description of the School District and Community

Center City Consolidated Schools is in the middle of the county in a northern state. The district serves three small communities and the surrounding farmlands. It is primarily a rural district including four elementary schools, a middle school, and a single high school. The district employs approximately 550 staff members of all types. The teaching staff averages 16.1 years of teaching experience.

Nearly all of the teachers hold masters degrees. Most of the teachers have computers at home. The district has invested a great deal into creating a strong technology program focusing on preparing children for the future world of work. A recent bond issue included significant funding for technology. Each classroom has at least one computer and all computers in the district are networked to the Internet. The area is largely agricultural and the economy in the area has not flourished for the past ten years. The largest single employer in the area, HelpData, is a firm that supports a range of CAD based software programs. However, due to the technical nature of the positions, many area residents are not able to obtain these positions, and a small but growing number of commuters are beginning to work in the area.

HelpData requires that all new employees in the support and technical areas of the business can type at 40 w.p.m. or faster.

The Background

Six years ago, the Board of Education, following the direction of a board member who worked in HelpData's human resources department, instituted a keyboarding graduation requirement. At the time, there was a fair amount of conversation about adding such a requirement. In the end, the Board voted 5 to 2 to add the requirement. Since then, several students and their parents had complained about the keyboarding requirement and more than a dozen students had to put off their graduation parties until after summer school in August.

However, the requirement has significantly impacted the number of local citizens hired by HelpData and non-college bound students are getting good jobs without having to move out of town. The graduation rate of non-college bound students has risen by approximately ten percent to nearly 85% in the last four years since a diploma nearly guarantees a job at HelpData. The Business Education Department is also very supportive of the requirement since their staffing levels have risen with the need for everyone to take a keyboarding course.

Detractors complain that the school district is catering too much to HelpData. In addition, they feel the 40 w.p.m. requirement is simply too high for the average high school graduate. They have seen a number of students take additional keyboarding courses as opposed to AP courses to prepare for the senior year keyboarding test. The technology coordinator is also concerned that keyboarding speed is too much of a focus and that the other technology skills students should have are being ignored.

The Assignment

The high school principal comes to the cabinet meeting after the seniors' keyboarding exams and says he has a problem. The potential valedictorian of the class failed the keyboarding exam. The student in question has already been accepted to Harvard on a full academic scholarship. In the past, students who failed the exam had to wait until after the graduation ceremony to retake it. So, they graduated in August at the end of summer school. The valedictorian would then not graduate first in the class and his scholarship could be in serious jeopardy. However, if the principal makes a change in the rules, the students ranking two and three in the class will be upset about their change in status. The principal asked the cabinet what to do. The superintendent then directed you as the assistant superintendent for curriculum to recommend a well-researched plan of action he can take to the Board of Education. The superintendent also reminds you that he wants a long-term recommendation as to whether or not to keep or possibly modify the keyboarding requirement as well.

Potential Resources

Bennett, L. (2001). Technology standards for the preparation of teachers, *International Journal of Social Education, 15*(2) 1-11.

Callison, D. (2002). Scope and sequence, *School Library Media Activities Monthly, 18*(7), 35-40+.

Dugger, W. E. (2002). Standards for technological literacy, *Tech Directions, 61*(8) 27-31.

Eisenberg, M. B. (2001). Beyond the bells and whistles: Technology skills for a purpose, *MultiMedia Schools, 8*(3), 44-48+.

Illinois Technology Standards available at http://talent.ed.uiuc.edu/docs/IllinoisStateTechnologyStandards.pdf.

ISTE's National Educational Technology Standards for Teachers (NETS) available at http://www.iste.org/standards/.

Johnson, Doug. *The Indispensable Teacher's Guide to Computer Skills*, 2nd edition. Worthington, OH: Linworth Publishing.

Technology Skills and Implementation for Teachers available at http://profiler.scrtec.org/smf/survey.jsp?survey_id=1354.

Zhao, J. J. & Alexander, M. W. (2002). Information technology skills recommended for business students by Fortune 500 executives, *Delta Pi Epsilon Journal, 44*(3), 175-89.

Chapter 5

Library Programming

Your Job Is on the Line

Description of the District

You are the district school library media director of a large semi-urban school district. You serve three high schools, seven middle schools, and fifteen elementary schools. In addition, you manage a central processing center for materials and a district-wide film and video library. The city and towns encompassed by the district are generally working class communities and the taxes are not keeping up with the growth. The district has not been able to pass a tax rate increase in the last decade although they have tried four times. All areas of the communities are being stretched to the limit and the Board is taking a critical look at all expenses.

In the past six years, class sizes at the elementary schools have gone up to over 28 students in the average class. Most high school classes are at or above 30 students. Six years ago, the average high school class size was 23 and elementary classes ranged from 18 to 24. The district has implemented a "pay to play" policy for athletics in order to retain all of its middle school and high school athletic teams. The district is seriously considering further classroom teacher cuts and eliminating elementary foreign language programs in the three elementary schools that have such programs.

The Background

The new superintendent and the current Board of Education are very focused on site-based management as a way to manage the district. The superintendent has already cut the entire staff development department at the district level and most of the technology staff other than the bare-bones network administrator positions. This round of cuts is looking particularly grim again. Especially since you are one of the few district level coordinators left intact. Your department has escaped any cuts to date due to the central processing services. For whatever reason, they had been clearly defined as required in the district's previous teachers' contract. The requirement to provide them was removed from the contract two years ago, but the department has still not been cut or reduced.

Currently, you have a staff of seven; two catalogers, three processing aides, a secretary, and a van driver who delivers the materials and provides for inter-library loan services between all of the buildings and the public libraries as well. The public libraries pay 62% of the driver's salary. Your staff also maintains a district-wide union catalog that is available via the Internet to the entire community.

Due to the lack of clerical assistance in the school library media centers, the SLMSs generally have told you that they could not process their own materials if the processing center was closed. Currently, most materials are arriving pre-processed and the catalogers are mostly cleaning up records and making sure the union catalog is accurate and complete. The processing aides are also responsible for servicing the district's textbook program that you manage.

You are also responsible for coordinating the K-12 information literacy program throughout the district, but in reality, you are only given three meetings a year with all of the school library media specialists. So, although there is a curriculum in place, it varies widely from school to school.

At the last district administrative retreat, nearly all of the building principals articulated that they would like to decide at the building level whether or not to obtain services from your department. If they didn't "purchase" your services, they could use those funds however they choose at the building level. The building SLMS were outraged by what they felt was a total lack of support by their principals.

The Assignment

Your direct supervisor, the assistant superintendent for operations, asks you to put together a memo detailing the advantages of maintaining centralized cataloging services and library media leadership. You are asked also to articulate the advantages and disadvantages of moving to site-based management of the individual school library media programs.

Additional Information

When you told your peers in other districts about your assignment, they sent you the following e-mails to help you out.

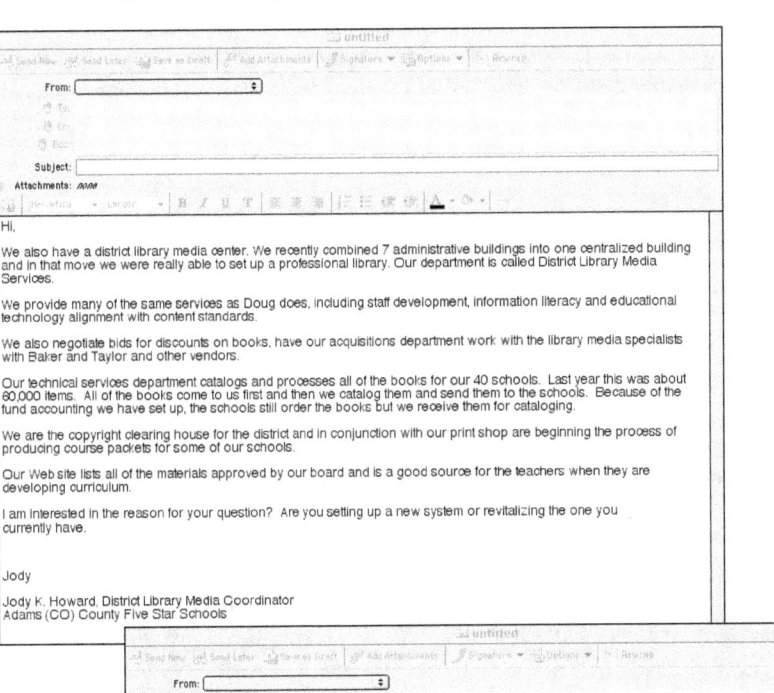

Hi,

We also have a district library media center. We recently combined 7 administrative buildings into one centralized building and in that move we were really able to set up a professional library. Our department is called District Library Media Services.

We provide many of the same services as Doug does, including staff development, information literacy and educational technology alignment with content standards.

We also negotiate bids for discounts on books, have our acquisitions department work with the library media specialists with Baker and Taylor and other vendors.

Our technical services department catalogs and processes all of the books for our 40 schools. Last year this was about 60,000 items. All of the books come to us first and then we catalog them and send them to the schools. Because of the fund accounting we have set up, the schools still order the books but we receive them for cataloging.

We are the copyright clearing house for the district and in conjunction with our print shop are beginning the process of producing course packets for some of our schools.

Our Web site lists all of the materials approved by our board and is a good source for the teachers when they are developing curriculum.

I am interested in the reason for your question? Are you setting up a new system or revitalizing the one you currently have.

Jody

Jody K. Howard, District Library Media Coordinator
Adams (CO) County Five Star Schools

Hi,

I am forwarding your question to the SPVS Division of AASL. I believe your question is a good one that all of us should be asking. With books coming already processed, online sources of cataloging, video production done at the desktop, and a variety of other "district" services now seeming to be done more at the building level, plus strained school budgets, we're all wondering about this.

Mankato district media services still:
- Facilitates district-wide information literacy and technology curriculum writing
- Does long-range planning for libraries and technology (including PR and marketing)
- Does staff development for teachers, administrators, secretaries, and media specialists
- Facilitates previews of instructional support materials (videos, software, on-line resources)
- Manages district Web site
- Manages all e-mail accounts and staff and student on-line file storage
- Sets up IP controlled access to on-line databases and other on-line subscription resources
- Consolidates and does final processing of library book orders and textbooks
- Organizes bar-code distribution
- Maintains the automation systems, Web interfaces to them, and multi-library search engine
- Manages the library budgets
- Has a video film collection it distributes
- Runs a print shop for large orders
- Maintains a laminator, poster maker, etc.
- Does minimal video copying and editing
- And probably other stuff I've now forgotten

Of course, our department handles all the technology "stuff" in the district, including the student information systems, WAN, e-mail, web, etc. and coordinates the work of the building techs.

Thanks for posting the question and I look forward to reading the responses.

Doug

Doug Johnson
Director of Media and Technology
I.S.D. 77, Mankato Public Schools

Potential Resources

Few resources speak to this issue directly. However, the items below will help you determine the issues involved.

Adcock, D. C., Ed. (1999). A Planning Guide for Information Power: Building Partnerships for Learning with School Library Media Program Assessment Rubric for the 21st Century. (The AASL Line Series). Chicago: American library Association.

Guide for Developing and Evaluating School Library Media Programs. (2000). Englewood, CO: Libraries Unlimited, 6th Edition.

Jones, P. A. (2003). The executive briefing, Knowledge Quest, 32(2), 30-34.

Katchel, D.E. (2003). Partners for success: A school library advocacy training program for principals, Knowledge Quest, 32(2), 30-34.

Latrobe, K. & Masters, A. (1999). Assessing the library media program and its partnerships: the implementation of Information Power, Teacher Librarian; 27(2), 8-13, December.

Ohlrich, K. B. (1996). What are we? Library media information specialists, computer technology coordinators, teacher instructional consultants, school-based management team members, or what? School Library Media Activities Monthly; 12(9), 26-28+, May.

Wilkinson, G. L. (1996). Library media standards and guidelines: a survey of resources for K-12 program planning and evaluation. Educational Media and Technology Yearbook, 21, 136-52.

To Build or Not to Build: That Is the Question

Description of the District

You have been hired as a consultant for a medium sized far-suburban school district. It was a nearly rural district only five years ago and is now in the process of growing quickly due to suburban sprawl. The towns encompassed by the district are generally conservative and the taxes are not keeping up with the growth. All areas of the communities are being stretched to the limit by the growth, causing each taxing body to take a critical look at all expenses. The new businesses in the area tend to be technology related including one very large health care software company that provides nearly 1,200 local jobs. The district does pride itself on its state test scores and the local realtors are strongly in favor of maintaining good schools in order to keep home values as high as possible.

The Background

The staff has been asked to participate in considering cost reductions related to building two new schools, an elementary school housing grades K-5 and a middle school housing grades 6-8. The staff has really worked hard to try to contain costs, but there has also been a great deal of angst and division among the staff. In effect two camps has arisen regarding the new schools and how dollars should be saved. The one position is trying to eliminate a second gymnasium at the new middle school in order to save enough money to include a large library media and technology center in the new building. The advocates of this program articulate the need for a strong library media program. They are referencing the Colorado Study and similar research to support their view.

The other group of teachers, including a number of classroom teachers eager to obtain more technology within their classrooms are forwarding the argument that the library is no longer needed. With so much information available on the Internet, the classroom teachers can provide much better instruction in research than a single school librarian. This would be especially true if the school district would redirect the computers that would go into the proposed library and put them into the classrooms so teachers had more direct access to additional computers.

You have been brought in to help the district's top administrators and Board of Education decide what to do. There is clear evidence that the previous library programs in the district have been under-whelming. The district has had a difficult time finding qualified school library media specialists and has in the past hired a number of uncertified SLMS due to a lack of certified applicants. However, Nixon Elementary School has been blessed with an excellent SLMS and its program has been recognized by the state educational media association as an excellent program. Nixon's test scores in reading are also above the district's average even though they have a higher than average low-income population at the school.

The district also has a history of eliminating elementary libraries at two of the other elementary schools when they were in dire need of classroom space over the past two years. However, in each of those cases, the SLMS was retained to still work with classes in regular classrooms and provide planning time for the primary teachers. Those cases were clearly identified as temporary until the last new school was built and those libraries have been reopened, but due to overcrowding, they may again be made into classrooms. This time, however, the SLMS positions will most likely be reduced to part time, if retained at all. So those in favor of the middle school library/technology center are deeply worried that the district may soon have no library media program at all.

The district's technology director is also eager to take over the funds presently allocated for print materials. During the times when the other libraries were closed, the print materials budgets were given over to the technology department for online services and software. The technology director is strongly lobbying to get the print material funds moved under his auspices so he can "better manage" access to all types of instructional support materials. The library staff is expressing concern that such a move would effectively eliminate any new print materials being purchased with direct district funds.

The Assignment

You are to articulate in a white paper to the superintendent and Board of Education what you feel are the advantages and disadvantages of eliminating the library technology center (LTC) or retaining it in the new middle school.

Additional Information

The third grade test scores from the elementary schools for the last five years. A score of 45 is the state average. A score of 50 is considered above standards. Carter and Clinton both had their library media centers closed in SY 2000 and SY 2001.

Figure 5.1 Third Grade Test Scores

School Year	Carter	Clinton	Johnson	Nixon	Thompson
SY 1999	45	51	50	48	45
SY 2000	46	48	49	49	46
SY 2001	39	45	53	50	44
SY 2002	37	44	52	52	38
SY 2003	39	43	51	54	39

Figure 5.2: Current Plan for Technology at the New Middle School

	With LTC	Without LTC
Classroom Computers	3	6
Printers	0	1
Video Projectors	1 per 2 classrooms	1 in each classroom
Gym space	1 gym	2 gyms
Technology teacher	1	1
Technology aides	3	2
SLMS	1	0
Print collection	7 books per student	No general print collection
Magazine collection	22 periodical titles	All materials to be online

Potential Resources

Asselin, M. (2003). Improving literacy education through professional study: The leadership role of the teacher-librarian, Teacher Librarian. 31(1), 53.

Asselin, M. (2003). Assessment issues and recommendations, Teacher Librarian. 30(5), 52-56.

Everhart, N. (2003). Evaluation of school library media centers: Demonstrating quality, Library Media Connection, 21 (6), 14-16.

Everhart, N. (2003). Controversial issues in school librarianship. Worthington, OH: Linworth.

Hartzell, G. (2003). Change? Who me? School Library Journal, 49 (3), 41.

Hopkins, D. M. (1996). The Library Bill of Rights and school library media programs, Library Trends, 45(1), 61-62.

Loertscher, D. & Woolls, B. (2003). A true assessment of your program's value. School Library Journal, June. 49(6), S3.

Library Degree Not Required

Description of the School District

You are one of three library media specialists in the Albacore-Nigel Unified School District. The Albacore-Nigel Unified School District is a rural district in a western state. The district houses approximately 800 K-12 students in three attendance centers. Most students ride the bus for 30 to 45 minutes both to and from school. The communities served by the district are all small farming communities, and agriculture is the industrial staple as well. The largest industry in the area is a small meat packing plant in the eastern edge of the district. The district remains largely white in demographics, however a small but growing Hispanic population has appeared in the district over the last five years.

The district's three schools are all in need of minor repair. The oldest building is the Albacore Attendance Center for K-4 students. The core of that structure actually dates to 1926 making it the first multi-room school house in the county. The Nigel and Custer Attendance Centers are slightly more modern. Nigel School was built as a technical trade school in 1934 as a Works Project Administration project and Custer School was built in 1948 as the Custer Secondary School. It serves as the present 9-12 high school.

The ANUSD has a very tight budget, as do many rural schools across the nation. The district had had to resort to pay-to-play athletics and eliminate some of the smaller activities programs due to budget constraints in the last five years. The teachers are unionized, but the educational support personnel and bus drivers are not.

The Background

In the past, ANUSD has always had a strong library program. Part of this was due to the former superintendent being married to a library school professor. However, two years ago, the superintendent moved to another state to be the superintendent in a larger district. The new superintendent's background does not have a rich library media tradition. The district is looking to find additional cost savings. The new superintendent set up a Cost Containment Committee to look at all aspects of the district and determine additional ways of saving money without cutting programs.

The Cost Containment Committee's report was released to staff as a whole yesterday. You were shocked to see that committee report stated that eliminating two of the three certified school library media positions was near the top of their list. Your two peers are both retiring at the end of the year. The committee has suggested that paraprofessional aides could replace them and that you could oversee all three library programs from your vantage point at the high school. Other districts in the area have similar programs in place.

Part of the problem with this reduction in staff is the fact the other two school library media specialists are both retiring, so no one has to be let go to realize this cost savings. In addition, the district will claim, as some other area district have that it is unable to find any qualified candidates. No one on the faculty currently has a library media endorsement except for the three of you.

The Assignment

The superintendent and the business manager have requested that everyone potentially affected by the Cost Containment Committee report put together a response. You are to explain your position as to the impact on your program and if you disagree with the suggestions, how else you could reduce your program. Also, what impact would your program incur if the proposed cut were made at 25%, 50%, or 125% of that suggested by the committee. Since your two colleagues are leaving at the end of the year, they feel you should take the lead on putting this presentation together.

Additional Information

Figure 5.3 Items Suggested to be cut by the Cost Containment Committee.

Department	Item/Program	Potential Savings
Administration	Eliminate one administrative position	$85,000
	Eliminate treats at faculty meetings	$2,300
	Replace switchboard operator with automated attendant	$17,500
Academics	Eliminate elective automotives program	$245,000+
	Eliminate driver education program	$323,000
	Reduce the counseling staff by one	$45,000
	Replace retiring librarians with aides	$50,000
Athletics	Eliminate all freshman athletic teams	$47,000
	Increase ticket price for all home events	?

Figure 5.4: ANUSD Library Budget

Salaries and benefits (3 SLMS, 1 aide)	$188,000
Print materials	$4,500
Electronic subscriptions	$7,500
Audio-visual materials	$2,500
Periodicals	$2,100
Supplies	$450
Professional Development	$300
Equipment	$2,750

Potential Resources

Most of the following resources deal with the current and expanding roles of para-professionals in educational and library settings. Materials on the value of certified library media staffing can generally be found in national and state library media standards including Information Power.

American Association of School Librarians and Association for Educational and Communications Technology. (1998). Information Power: Building Partnerships for Learning. Chicago: American Library Association.

Davidson-Arnott, F. & Kay, D. (1998). Library technician programs: Skills-oriented paraprofessional education, Library Trends, 46(3), 540-63.

Farmer, L. S. J. (2001). Teaming with Opportunity: Media Programs, Community Constituencies, and Technology. Englewood, CO: Libraries Unlimited.

French, N. K. (2003). Managing Paraeducators in Your School: How to Hire, Train, and Supervise Non-Certified Staff. Thousand Oak, CA: Corwin Press.

Kalnin, M. T. (1997). Some thoughts on role-blurring and staff development, Library Mosaics; 8(6), 8-10.

Leonhardt, T. W. (1996). Keys to success for library paraprofessionals and support staff, Library Administration & Management, 10(4), 214-19.

Lichtenstein, A. A. (1999). Surviving the information explosion: Training paraprofessionals for reference service, Journal of Educational Media & Library Sciences, 37(2), 125-34.

Porterfield, D. M. (1997). The plight of the paraprofessional: Second-class citizens or untapped resource? Library Mosaics, 8(4), 8-10.

Smallwood, C. (1999). Training student and adult assistants, interns, and volunteers: Tips for new librarians servicing small libraries, Book Report, 17(4), 24-26.

Tin, K. L. & Al-Hawamdeh, S. (2002). The changing role of paraprofessionals in the knowledge economy, Journal of Information Science, 28(4), 331-43.

Chapter 6

Planning and Program Evaluation

The Accountant-less Audit

Description of the School District and Community

Lone Cloud Community School District is a medium sized district with approximately 1,200 students in four school buildings. It is in a suburban/rural area and the schools cover three small towns. The district employs 143 staff members of all types. You have a wide area network and each building is networked. The MIS systems that are in place are relatively old. Some are still character-based. Most provide basic functionality, but they are probably in need of review. Each school has computers in most classrooms, but some of the computers are more than five years old. Each school has a centralized software inventory, but teachers also bring in their own programs from home. The district's test scores are a little lower than one would expect for a suburban district, but in the past that has been blamed on a growing migrant Hispanic population and a large special education program.

Lone Cloud Community School District has come under new leadership. Dr. Jo Hollingsworth has been brought in to be an agent of change. The school board feels that there are a number of areas in which the district is lagging behind. You are the technology director and at least so far, the board has not been concerned about technology. Dr. Jo's secretary called you today and has asked to set up an appointment to discuss a technology audit of the district. She wants you to bring in an outline of the areas that should be assessed and what key questions should be asked regarding each facet of technology in the school district.

The Assignment

Prepare a memo that the superintendent can share with the board that outlines the areas you believe should be included in the upcoming technology audit. Include a rationale for why each issue should be addressed.

Exhibit One

The following audit questions were taken from the *Reuter's Guide to Good Information Strategy* and sent to you by the business manager when he heard about your assignment. The questions focus on the business of schools, but not as much on the instructional components.

- *What technologies are in place?*
- *Which of these are stand-alone and which are integrated?*
- *Could any cost or efficiency benefits be obtained by integrating stand-alone systems?*
- *Could any archaic IT or even paper based information systems be improved by technological changes?*
- *Would the organization benefit from a system that enables people to extract knowledge from their corporate data, such as a data warehouse?*
- *Are individuals hampered in their search for information by a slow or unsatisfactory network? Would this situation be alleviated by a systems upgrade?*
- *Are employees properly trained to use systems correctly and efficiently?*
- *Could payback times be calculated for desired technology upgrades?*

Exhibit Two

A local technology director shared the following list of facets to have your auditor review. A consultant auditing her technology program used the same list.

- *Installed hardware base*
- *Network infrastructure*
- *Software*
- *Administrative systems*
- *Telephone systems*
- *Staff development programs*
- *Policy management*
- *Internet presence*
- *IT management*

Potential Resources

Bell, R.J. et al. (1992). *Technology audit: Methodology and case study.* Paper presented at the Technology Transfer and Implementation Conference, July 1992. Available at http://www.oxin.co.uk/downloads/taudit.pdf.

Biggs, P. (1998). *Create Ownership in Your Long Range Plan with a Technology Audit, Computing Teacher,* 16(2), 31-33.

Bullock, C. & Ory, J. (2000). *Evaluating instructional technology implementation in a higher education environment, American Journal of Evaluation;* 21(3), 315-28.

CELT Corporation. *Available at http://www.celtcorp.com/home.htm.*

Edwards, C. E. (2002). *Reflections on "A framework for quality in educational technology programs," Educational Technology,* 42(3), 29-32. May-June.

Eib, B.J. (2001). *Beyond the bells and whistles: Evaluating technology use in the classroom, Principal Leadership,* 1(9),16-23 May-June.

Gardner, H. B. (2000). *Technology Audits...Grappling with Accountability. TECHNOS,* 9 (4), 10-13.

Michael, S. O. (1998). *Best Practices in Information Technology (IT) Management: Insights from K-12 Schools' Technology Audits. International Journal of Educational Management;* 12(6), 277-88.

Online guide to evaluating information technology. (2001). Converge Magazine, 4(5), 42.

Schwering, R.E. (2002). *The IT Audit Assignment: Viewing Technology in the Organizational and Strategic Context, Journal of Management Education,* 26(4), 344-55.

Sydow, J.A. & Kirkpatrick, C. M. (1996). *A Technology Checkup, School Administrator,* 53(4), 15-17.

Also search the Internet using such terms as "technology audit" and "review of technology systems."

The White Elephants

Description of the School

You are the technology coordinator for the Columbus Preparatory School. It is a private school for 6th to 12th graders; many of them have troubled backgrounds. The school presently enrolls approximately 750 students. The staff includes approximately 70 teachers and another 20 support staff. The school's president, Dr. Laura Pasquale, strives to keep the school's ACT and SAT scores higher than any of the local public schools. Similarly, she works hard to hire and retain excellent teachers. All of this is done on a shoestring budget.

The Background

The school has approximately 300 computers. Many are out of date, but they all perform the functions they were purchased for and are used regularly and effectively. The computers are all PCs; although there is a wide range of types of machines. The oldest machines are still able to run Windows 98. Many are running Windows 2000. All are networked on an Ethernet network.

Dr. Pasquale has recently spoken to you about trying to find some new computers for you. She is always trying to find a great deal on things for the school. In fact, if she has a fault, it is her desire to get a "great deal" for the school. In the past, she purchased several old printers for you that were basically useless, but you made a show out of thanking her for them and hooking them up to the network. Within two months all of the printers were in the dumpster. It took more than 45 hours of time to get them set up and troubleshoot them before they made it to the dumpsters.

This time, Dr. Pasquale comes to you very excited about obtaining some new computers. A parent works at a bank that is about to replace their computers and has 45 computers to donate. She asks you to call the bank and find out more about her find.

When you call the bank's IT director, Sam Rosen, he tells you that the bank would love to bring the computers to you. They are old, but functional. However, there are some drawbacks you should know about. The bank has erased all of the hard drives and they no longer have the original system software for the machines. In addition, the machines are six years old and were built by a local computer store that has gone out of business. They only have Token ring network cards in them.

Ethernet cards would have to be added. Some of the monitors are actually 8 to 9 years old, and some are actually black and white. Most of them work okay according to Sam. Sam also tells you some of the floppy drives are finicky, but they usually work. Only a few of the machines have CD-ROM drives. He wonders why you want them, but is more than willing to give them to you so as not to have to pay for disposal.

The Assignment

When you go back to Dr. Pasquale's office, what do you tell her? How will you be able to rationalize that this find is not really the diamond in the rough she thinks it is?

Additional Question

How would you change your answer, if at all, to Dr. Pasquale if she offered you 45 sets of 1995 *World Book Encyclopedias* instead of the computers?

Potential Resources

Graef, R., et al. (1990). Selection skills and collection development in school libraries, Book Report; 9(2), 14-15+.

Monroe (WA) Montessori School.(2003). Monroe Montessori School Donation Policy. Available at http://www.monroemontessori.com/PBC/Donation_policy.htm.

Our Lady of Good Counsel Parish. (2003). New technology donation policy. Available at http://school.olgc.org/donate.html.

Sherman, G. & Knox, D. (1981). Media selection policies for private schools, School Library Journal, 28(2), 109.

Also search the Internet for information about library selection and donation policies.

Creating a CIO

Description of the District

You are the assistant superintendent for human resources for a large suburban school district. The district has eighty-seven schools including twelve high schools. The district recently came about through the merger of three smaller districts, which had been originally formed in 1876 with the implementation of the state's new school law. The Board of Education and the superintendent had tried fairly hard to bring a single culture to the new district, but such work was only partially successful. The old "city district" maintained its preeminence since it was squarely in the center of the district and the majority of the central administration came from its ranks. Retirements and some pre-merger flight in the other two districts contributed to the overabundance of city district administrators.

Overall, the district has done well through the merger. The taxes in the outlaying areas have been slightly reduced by the additional revenues provided by the downtown city businesses. The district has struggled to bring three separate infrastructures into a single unified whole. The phone systems are still not together and the networks are bridged together using VPN technology. They are not tied directly together at this point. Software is relatively standard throughout the district, but a wide range of software variety can be found from school to school and there is no complete inventory. To be direct, there isn't even anything close to a complete inventory.

Technology is divided up into a number of departments at the present. The business office under the executive director for finance manages the network and data infrastructure. The assistant superintendent for educational services is responsible for instructional technology and classroom integration. Library services are also under educational services. The telephone systems are managed by the maintenance department under the direction of the assistant superintendent for operations. The executive director for administration is responsible for the district's Web site. You are responsible for technology staff development as part of the human resources department.

There is very little centralized management of technology and most of the cabinet level administrators supervising these areas know little about the day to day management of what are increasingly becoming mission critical functions to the district. The assistant superintendent for educational services is the only administrator who seems desirous of maintaining his oversight of technology related areas. The others all seem at best to be neutral as to whether or not they would retain control of technology areas. The executive director for administration is eager to give management of the Web site. Presently, most of the Web work is outsourced and he hates dealing with the Web vendors.

Last year, the curriculum department purchased $45,000 of software for elementary computer labs in new schools. However, the software would not work on the new computers purchased for the labs in those schools. Generally, every area of technology can articulate one or more similar situations over the past six years. Only the administrative and payroll systems seem to be immune from these problems. One of the reasons for this is that the data processing manager who oversees those systems and the food service systems was originally hired as a consultant to integrate the three separate data systems. The district saw her skill and hired her out of retirement to manage the district's data systems.

The Assignment

The superintendent and the Board of Education have asked you to review the district's organization with regard to technology. The data processing manager has partially served to trigger this issue since she has announced she needs to retire in the next twelve months since her significant other is finally retiring.

The superintendent has asked you to determine how technology should be organized for the district. He has told you to review any and all reasonable options. Come up with a job description and an organizational chart for technology. He wants you to compile a listing of pros and cons for each option. If you create a new technology department, he would like to know what aspects of technology should be encompassed by the new department and what, if any, aspects of technology should remain under their present administrators. He also expects that you will need to create new job descriptions for any technology management positions under a CIO or whomever else each option puts in charge of technology. The Board's preference is to have one person responsible for at least the technical aspects of technology at the cabinet level.

The superintendent has asked for a short summary of the pros and cons of each option in a table format he can share with the board. He also wants an organizational chart for each option showing what functional areas are under each cabinet administrator. He wishes you luck and reminds you that the next board meeting is only three weeks away.

Additional Information

The following job description is for the chief information officer in a similar district elsewhere in the state.

Jerome Community School District R-14
Office of Personnel and Communications

Position/Title: Assistant Superintendent for Information Technology

Responsible to: Superintendent

Supervises: IT Managers/ IT & Library Department Chairs
Web Developers
Secretary

General Responsibilities:
The Assistant Superintendent for Information Technology provides technology direction for the district through the development and implementation of the District Technology Plan. The Assistant Superintendent is responsible for district-wide leadership of all information support programs, including the budget, daily operations, technology professional development, and supervision of staff. The Assistant Superintendent leads the instructional technology, information technology, and library programs.

Principal Duties:

- Develops and implements the long-range technology plans for the district.

- Leads the development and implementation of all academic and administrative budgetary and human resources related to technology.

- Directs the management of the district's technology infrastructure and support system, including assessing administrative and instructional technology needs, implementing program services, and monitoring and evaluating service delivery.

- Directs the instructional technology curricular program through supervision of the Instructional Technology Department Chair, and serves as liaison with the Assistant Superintendent for Curriculum and Instruction.

- Directs the library program and the development of information literacy and research skills throughout the curriculum through supervision of the Library Department Chair.

- Directs the development and modification of the district's technology staff development programs to meet specific district needs.

- Advises district administrators and teachers on planning and implementing curriculum with technology integration.

- Serves on the Board of Education's negotiations team in bargaining with staff associated with the Educational Support Personnel Association.

- Manages technology-related state and federal grants, including identifying needs, writing grant proposals, and monitoring grant implementation.

- Serves as the district's technology liaison to the community.

- Performs all other duties as assigned by the superintendent.

The options another district reviewed when determining how to replace their director of technology after his retirement.

Options for the Director of Information Technology Position

Option 1:
Retain all facets of the present position:
- Network infrastructure and help desk functions
- MIS functions
- Web development
- Telephone services
- Staff development program
- Instructional technology courses for students
- Library and audio-visual services

Option 2:
Remove the library program

Option 3:
Remove all certified staff supervision, moving IT courses into Technology Education Department

Retaining:
- Network infrastructure and help desk functions
- MIS functions
- Web development
- Telephone services
- Staff development program

The organizational chart they eventually settled upon.

Information Technology Department — Option A

- Director of Information Technology
  - Systems Analyst
  - Network Manager
  - Manager of Telecommunications
  - Instructional Technology Coordinator
  - Instructional Technology Dept. Chair
  - Systems Programmer
  - Systems Coordinator
  - Assistant Network Manager
  - 2.8 Technology Staff Developer/Teacher
  - System Support Specialist
  - Network Administrator
  - Help Desk Operator
  - 2 Web Developers
  - WAN Administrator
  - Inventory Control Specialist
  - Inventory Control
  - Web Database Developer
  - Video Engineer
  - 4 Computer Repair Specialists
  - Computer Repair Specialist
  - Secretary to the Director
  - Software Specialists

Potential Resources

Barber, B. (2002). The chief information officer. Job and organization design in the community college. ERIC document, ED474194.

Klinger, D. (2000). Herding Cats. Business Officer; November, 36-38.

Managing information technology as catalyst of change. (1994). ERIC document, ED398260.

Penrod, J.I, Dolence, M.G. & Douglas, J.V. (1990). The Chief Information Officer in Higher Education

Penrod, J. I. (2003). Creating a realistic IT vision: The roles and responsibilities of a chief information officer, Technology, Jan.-Feb.

Rowe, R. R. (1987). You, the CIO: Can Librarians Make the Jump to "Chief Information Officer"? American Libraries; 18(4), 297.

Zastrocky, M. R. & Schlier, F. (2000). The higher education CIO in the 21st century. Educause Quarterly, 23 (1) April, 53-59.

Assessing Your Own District

The District

You are the chief information officer for the Shirland Unified School District in a moderate sized university town on the west coast. The district consists of twelve elementary schools, four middle schools, two high schools, and an alternative secondary school. The district includes approximately 1,100 employees, nearly all are members of a collective bargaining unit.

All of the schools perform well on the state's academic tests. Approximately 85% of the students in the district continue their educations at four-year colleges or universities. Another 5% go to two-year colleges or trade schools. Approximately 5% also enlist in the military. The demographics of the district include nearly 20% African-American students, 32% Asian students, 20% Hispanic students, and 28% Caucasian and Native American. The district's poverty rate is approximately 12% percent based upon free and reduced lunch programs.

The Background

For the past four years, the superintendent and the Board of Education have given you the universal support to create a world-class technology program for the school district. You have been able to replace nearly all of the district's computers, hire additional staff for technical support and staff development. You have replaced the district's administrative systems in anticipation of meeting Y2K compliance. Your efforts ensured that the district had no Y2K issues. The district's Web presence has won national recognition in the past two years.

The superintendent and Board of Education are interested in being able to quantify the changes that they have supported with regard to technology. They have asked you to prepare a report showing where the district is regarding technology. They also want to know where they are in relationship to the other area school districts. The superintendent suggests you show where the district is on a continuum in each area that you address.

The Assignment

Create an assessment rubric for all aspects of technology within the district. It is important that you are able to justify why each area is (and potentially is not) included within the scope of your eventual self-assessment.

Potential Resources

> Adcock, D. C., Ed. (1999). *A Planning Guide for Information Power: Building Partnerships for Learning with School Library Media Program Assessment Rubric for the 21st Century.* Chicago: American Library Association.
>
> Baule, S. M. (2001). *Technology Planning for Effective Teaching and Learning.* 2nd. Ed. Worthington, OH: Linworth.
>
> Edwards, C. E. (2002). Reflections on "A framework for quality in educational technology programs," *Educational Technology,* 42(3), 29-32 May-June.
>
> Haycock, K. (1998). *Foundations for Effective School Library Media Programs.* Englewood, CO: Libraries Unlimited.
>
> Johnson, D. (2001). What gets measured gets done: the importance of evaluating your library media program, *Book Report,* 20(2), 14-15 Sept.-October.
>
> Kramer, P. K. (2000). Linking for Learning: the Illinois school library program guidelines help library media specialists translate theory into practice, *School Library Media Activities Monthly,* 16(8), 23-25+ April.
>
> McNabb, M., Hawkes, M. & Rouk, U. (1999). *Evaluating the Effectiveness of Technology* in Proceedings of The Secretary's Conference on Educational Technology. Washington, D.C., July 12-13, 1999.
>
> Quinones, S., Kirshstein, R. & Loy, N. (1998). *An Educator's Guide to Evaluating the Use of Technology in Schools and Classrooms.* Washington, DC: American Institutes for Research.
>
> Thorpe, R. (2002). How should we think about educational technology programs, *Educational Technology,* 42(3), 21-24 May-June.
>
> Yesner, B. L. & Jay, H. (1998). *Operating and Evaluating School Library Media Programs: A Handbook for Administrators and Librarians.* New York: Neal-Schuman.

Also search the Internet for information on planning and evaluating educational technology.

Chapter 7

Additional Issues for Discussion

For each of the following short scenarios, determine how one might go about resolving the problem(s) presented and what resources you might use. All of these are issues that have occurred in school libraries, computer labs or technology centers in the past few years. Although the answers to some problems might seem obvious, there tend to be additional considerations in many of the cases that need to be weighed in the decision making process.

1. You are the school library media specialist in a middle school of approximately 950 students. A 6th grade teacher comes into the Learning Resource Center (LRC) and asks you for your help in determining whether or not a student's book report was plagiarized. How might you respond?

2. You are the new school library media specialist in a small junior high school. Each day when it rained, one of the physical education teachers, who is also the athletic director, came in and asked your predecessor to find a movie for him to show to his classes for the day. When he comes in and asks you for a movie and reminds you that classes are 50 minutes long. How might you respond?

3. You are the head librarian for a medium sized high school. The student activities director calls you first thing in the morning and asks you if you can come down to his office and delete all trace of where he had visited on the Web. You had just seen an e-mail from the district office reminding staff that they were going to start cracking down on those staff members who violated the district's AUP. How might you respond?

4. The principal calls you at home on Thursday night and asks you what time Saturday you might be available to come and set up her new computer. She just moved and needs you to get her computer working so she can work from home. As far as you know, it is her personal computer and not a school district computer. How might you respond?

5. You are the district's technology coordinator. The superintendent leaves you a voice mail message that forwards her son's computer questions. She asks you to call her son and help him solve his laptop problem. This is a frequent occurrence. However, you are not alone. The custodial manager has been asked to send staff over to rake leaves, etc. at the superintendent's home. How might you respond?

6. You are the school library media specialist for an elementary school. You are jarred awake on Martin Luther King Day by a phone call from a teacher in another school in the district. It is 8:05 a.m. and you have the day off. She tells you that she needs help formatting her son's eighth grade project. You are sure you do not know this person, but her name is in the faculty directory you keep by the phone. How might you respond?

7. You are the head librarian of a high school with two other certified library media specialists. You are new and have found one of your librarians to be excellent, Karen, but the other is close to worthless, Pattie. The one you find nearly worthless is also the past president of the teachers' union. The English department chair stops you in the lunchroom and tells you she is very upset with Pattie. She feels that Pattie is not helpful and several of her teachers have mentioned how difficult she is to work with. In the future, the English department only wants to work with you or Karen. Since the English department is nearly 75% of Instructional Materials Center (IMC) traffic, this will put a real strain on you and Karen. How might you respond?

8. You are the technology coordinator for a small high school. You have a staff of seven including a library staff of three. Two faculty members in charge of "school spirit" have complained to you that the technology staffers always sit alone at lunch. They don't mix in with the rest of the staff. Your technology staffers have meanwhile complained that people harangue them with no end of computer questions and want free home computer advice. They never let your staff eat in peace. How might you respond to the school spirit committee? To your own staff?

9. You are the head librarian for a high school in a two high school district. At the previous board meeting, the library program at the other high school came under serious fire as being overstaffed and not properly run. You have always believed that the district should have a more unified library program and you have had your differences with the other head librarian. In fact, you are not sure she is truly competent. One of the Board's most contentious members calls you and asks if you can tell him what is really going on in the other school's library program? How might you respond?

10. You are the technology coordinator for a high school. You suspect one of your staff members is spending more of her time in the office consulting for other districts than working for you. Phone records for the phone in her office show a few phone calls to other district offices. However, you suspect most of her correspondence is done via e-mail. What might you do?

11. Your principal walks through your library and sees a cart of new books that you have not yet processed. She asks you if she can take three of them home to review. They happen to be books you ordered for another teacher's specific unit that is due to start next week. You have worked hard with the teacher to find these new books and her unit relies heavily on a research assignment the students are going to be assigned. You know that in the past, the principal has not been very responsible for returning materials. In fact, she probably has ten overdue books right now. How might you respond?

12. A good friend of yours is a physical education teacher and the head basketball coach in your school. He is working on his master's degree, but is struggling with the coursework. He had come to you earlier asking for help in gathering materials for his final research paper. He comes back to you on the Friday prior to the paper being due and asks if you could help him write the paper. In fact, he wants you to help create the research since he never had time to do the study because of basketball season. The paper is due Tuesday. If he isn't done, he won't get his degree or his anticipated advance on the salary scale. How might you respond?

13. A second year teacher comes into your library resource center (LRC) and asks you for some help in putting together a list of resources for her upcoming herpetology unit. She knows that you are already very busy with senior research courses, but she says that she needs the materials in two days. The LRC policy is very clear; teachers need to give the LRC staff a week's notice to create research pathfinders. The LRC director has recently reminded the faculty as a whole that the one week notice is very important for the LRC staff to be able to budget their time. How might you respond?

14. Your principal asks you to give him a list of seven software programs that he needs to install on his home computer for work. You do not have any extra copies of the programs in question, and none of them are licensed in such a way that your principal could legally install them on his home computer without purchasing an additional copy. In fact, several are computer aided drafting/design (CAD) related programs that his wife, an architect, might want to use as home, but you cannot see why he might need them. How might you respond?

15. Your network manager calls you and asks you to take a help desk call. None of the four technicians in your high school will deal with this woman any more. In fact, the caller insists that the IT department has again changed her password. The network manager states to you that the password has not been changed and that nearly the whole IT staff knows it because the caller regularly forgets it. When you arrive at her office, she is emptying out her desk drawers into a box and muttering that if no one is going to help her, she will simply leave. Her computer has not been turned on. Her office mate is staring at you with a look of shock and disbelief. When you ask if you can turn her computer on, she tells you in an icy tone that she already has turned it on, but someone changed her password and they are trying to force her out of her job. She then leaves the office with her box. When you review the help desk log, she has called the help desk 14 times in the past week with password problems. How might you respond?

16. You are the director of technology for a large school district, but your office is in one of the high schools. Your network manager also works out of the same building. One morning, a teacher appears in your doorway to complain. She states that the network manager is incredibly rude and obnoxious. He told her he didn't have time to fix her home computer, even after she carted it into his office. She now tells you that you should fire him and that she wants her computer fixed. She bought the computer through a staff computer buy, so she feels the district needs to repair it for her. As she leaves your office, the phone rings. It is your network manager warning you she is on her way. He also tells you he snapped at her, but he was on the phone with one of the elementary buildings fixing a routing table error and she was making so much noise he had to tell his worker at the elementary school he would have to call back. When he found out her problem was with her home computer, he nearly killed her. How might you respond to the teacher? To your network manager?

17. Your predecessor as the school library media specialist is still working in the same school. However, she is now a biology teacher. It is not clear to you what happened to make her move back to a classroom, but you are pretty sure it was not her choice. However, she remains popular with the staff. While inventorying the televisions and VCRs in the school, you find a collection of videos, DVDs, and CD-ROMs in her classroom that are all marked as discarded from the LRC collection. However, even in just glancing at the titles for a minute, it is clear all of the best biology materials in the school are no longer in the LRC, but are in this classroom. You continue with your inventory, but are bothered by the fact that the school has three other biology teachers who don't have access to those resources. What might you do?

18. You are the technology and media director for a high school. Due to the size of the library, you have been able to create a small staff break room and lunch room in the rear of the library. Generally, the library and technology staffs have liked to be able to use it and have access to their own refrigerator, etc. Halfway through the year, one of your computer repairmen complains that two of your other staff members sit in the break room making eyes at each other and that it makes him uncomfortable. About two weeks later someone else makes a similar complaint. One of the two staff members in question is married, but you have also noticed a "closeness" between the two that seems to border on the inappropriate. How might you respond?

19. You have a new math teacher that is driving the IMC staff nuts. He is constantly bringing his classes into the library to work on Internet-based assignments, but most are generally worksheet quality assignments that require no higher order thinking skills. He is obviously the pet of the math and science division chair who knows nearly nothing about computers and hasn't brought his classes to the IMC or the adjacent computer lab in the past decade. Most assignments could be done using an atlas or an almanac. Your IMC staff want these assignments to stop since they are taking time from other teachers who they could be working with on information literacy skills. How might you respond?

20. You are the technology director of a fairly large district. You had just sent out a reminder to all staff that the computers will need to remain in the school over the summer so that the IT staff can upgrade each of them and re-clone them. The Board recently passed a policy requiring that the computers not be sent home with staff except for district business. You have an old friend who is still an elementary classroom teacher. She calls you up the next day, near the end of the school year, and asks if it would be okay if she takes her classroom computer and printer home for the summer. She is finishing her dissertation in educational administration and all of her work is on the school computer. She doesn't have a good computer at home and wants to use the school computer, if it is okay with you. She promises she won't tell anyone that she is borrowing the school's computer and that she promises to have it back before the school year starts. How might you respond?

21. You are the technology director for a small district. The previous superintendent who hired you just retired and is now teaching at a local university. Although your relationship wasn't close, you thought he was a good guy for the job. The new superintendent just took over on July 1. She had previously been the assistant superintendent for operations. She is a little paranoid by nature and she was surely not your choice for the job, but the Board didn't ask you your opinion before hiring her. She summons you into her office and asks if you can retrieve all of the previous superintendent's e-mail and files. She feels that she should review them in case some important information is in them that the previous superintendent did not share with her during the transition. You know that the previous superintendent did leave her a lot of documents, since you were the one who helped him go through his files. However, since he was not computer savvy he asked you not to delete any of his files for a year in case he missed something when he backed up his other documents. You also know he had a lot of personal e-mail come to the school's account since you often helped him with e-mail issues. How might you respond?

22. You are the head librarian for a very large high school. There are four library media specialists on the library staff. You have a new library media specialist that is not working out. However, she is very popular with the school staff. She is an excellent volleyball coach and is very visible at athletic contests, etc. However, she is just not a good librarian. All of the other library media specialists agree with you. When you speak with the principal about not retaining her for a second year, she tells you that you should really consider keeping her on. The principal thinks that she is an excellent coach and a great model for school spirit. How might you respond?

23. You are the technology and media director for a large district with over 400 staff members. The help desk coordinator is reviewing the monthly help desk statistics with you and points out two staff members as problems. One of the staff members is a very highly respected English teacher who usually reduces the help desk operator to tears screaming about some miniscule issue that in most cases ends up being a user error. She has called screaming seven times in the last two months. The other issue is a one-on-one special education aide. He doesn't even really use a computer that much for his job. However, he teaches a culinary arts class at a local community college and uses the school's computers to prepare most of his materials and handouts according to the help desk coordinator. He also does not understand technology at all. He has logged over 175 calls in the last two months alone. He is personally responsible for 8% of the districts' help desk call volume. The coordinator would like to know how you might help solve these two problems for the help desk staff? How would you respond?

24. You are the district's technology director. You just returned to your office from the monthly district administrative team meeting. You get a call from one of your building techs. She alerts you to the fact that one of the high school's deans has asked to have Solitaire put back onto his computer about seven times already in the first two days back to school. She warns you he will probably be contacting you next. When the computers were re-cloned this summer, you had Solitaire and other games removed from the master build, because a number of complaints came that secretaries were spending too much time playing games and not working at their desks. The dean in question had just mentioned the Solitarie issue to you at the team meeting after mentioning how busy he was as the school year was ramping up. The principal of the high school had been one of the key proponents of removing the games from the clone. How might you respond?

25. You are the assistant superintendent for technology in a moderate sized suburban school district. At the superintendent's weekly cabinet meeting, the director of operations brings in an architect who is going to lead the work to build a new high school. The superintendent introduces each of the cabinet members to the architect. When he introduces you, he mentions that you also supervise the district's library media program. The architect tells you he looks forward to working together to convince the "library ladies" that they really won't need much space for books in the new high school. After the meeting, you check up on the architect's references and discover that none of the libraries his firm has designed have been very functional, and most library media specialists have serious misgivings about the spaces his firm has designed. How might you respond?

26. You are the technology education department chair for a junior/senior high school. This year, you have a new female teacher who has a great deal of promise and technical skill. However, she is teaching nearly all 7-9th grade boys in basic computer courses. She is having a great many discipline problems. Some are the normal type any first year teacher might have. However, you are also concerned that some of the issues are raised because she wears very revealing clothing. Her skirts are short and her shirts and pants are too tight. You are concerned her clothing is probably distracting the young men in her class. How might you address the issue?

27. You are the chief information officer of a school district. Your network manager brings you her preferred candidate for a help desk position. She is a young, recently married woman. Both you and the director of human resources are pretty sure she is pregnant. The district has a very liberal maternity leave program that will give her ten weeks of paid leave without affecting her sick leave or vacation. She is surely the best candidate after you review the network manager's second and third choices. However, the director of human resources really feels that the young woman should not be hired since she will be going out on a long-term leave within a year. What do you do?

28. You are a library media specialist in a small, close knit elementary school. One of the primary teachers asks you if you will write a letter of recommendation for her to a graduate program in library science. You like the woman as a person and the two of you travel in the same social circles. However, you find her to be an adequate teacher at best. She has no control of her classroom and loves to drop students into the LMC at all times of day. Adding to your concern, she has not waived the right to review your reference on the sheet she gave you. How might you respond to her?

29. You are the new chief information officer of a flagship school district. Prior to your arrival in the district, the district used a consulting service that you felt was really overcharging the district for its IT services. You have not used the service since you took over. In fact, you effectively fired the company on your first day on the job. However, the company puts your district down as a reference on many school related proposals. You get a call from another CIO asking about the company. However, you were not listed a reference by the company. Your predecessor was listed. She was fired for incompetence. How do you respond?

30. You are the library media and technology director for a small private school. Your president invites you to a meeting of the Board of Trustees to discuss computer purchases. One of the trustees is concerned that the school is spending too much on computers. He notices in the weekly newspaper ads that computers can be purchased for much less than the name-brand computers that you are presently purchasing. You are presently purchasing Dell computers with a three-year warranty. He is suggesting you have a local computer store build computers for you instead and he feels you could save a great deal of money that way. Your president asks you to prepare to defend your present purchasing program at the next Board of Trustees meeting. How might you respond?

Chapter 8

Considerations for Resolving the Cases

For each of the cases presented in the book, there are some key considerations that must be considered in order to successfully complete the assignment presented in the case. There are no correct answers for any of the given cases. All of the cases need to be considered in the context of the school or district in which they occurred. One of the disadvantages of the case method is the lack of ability of the author to truly immerse one in the culture and personalities within a given school or district. The advantage of that drawback is that each reader will come to the case with their own unique perspective that has been forged by their own education and experiences. When case studies are discussed in classrooms or other professional settings, that diversity makes the case method that much richer.

In each of the short entries following, the key points or considerations of the cases have been highlighted for one's consideration. In no case are all of the issues presented in the case touched upon. Most of the cases presented have more information presented than necessary to respond to the key issue or issues in the case. In the same way, there is rarely enough information to eliminate any reasonable course of action. The key is to ground one's response in previous experience and basic management theory where experience is lacking.

The Filtering Follies

If one chooses to filter the staff machines, they need to consider that the staff may feel that they are not being treated as professionals. This is particularly true due to the proximity and interrelationship with the college faculty. However, one has to balance that with a duty to taxpayers. If one is using tax dollars to effectively allow staff access to sites that would be filtered for sex or violence, what message does that send to the community? If the students are filtered, why does the faculty need access to filtered sites? Those sites would not be able to be used with classes. The key issue is how to balance the staff's need for professionalism with the district's need to implement filtering.

Muggles, Muggles Everywhere

The key to this issue is to ensure that the process is clear and fair to the challenged material. Just as in a case involving a person, the materials need to be given due process. The culture of the school or district will influence the exact process, but the decision as to whether or not to retain the book or video should be made by a group as opposed to a single individual. The process should include classroom teachers, library media specialists, and administrators. Potentially parents and students could also be involved.

One other issue is that materials that are required for a course should be held to a higher standard than materials provided as supplemental to the instructional process. The process also needs to be clearly articulated so that all involved know how to respond to a potential challenge. In many cases, if a potential challenger needs to complete a thorough reconsideration form, the form will not be returned. Many challengers want to be able to simply provide an oral challenge and have the book or video immediately removed. Ensuring that cannot happen by having a clearly articulated process will help eliminate some potential challenges. Also consider that many challenges actually come from staff members both directly and indirectly.

Well, That Isn't Education Related!

In any personnel issue, one of the key issues is to assure that the staff member in question is given due process. The staff member must be given the opportunity to explain his side of the story and in most cases they have the right to either counsel or at least union representation. Do not begin any disciplinary proceedings until the staff member has been given the opportunity to obtain representation. Many educational labor issues are found in favor of staff members due to a procedural error on the part of the administration.

From a technical standpoint, it is important to be able to document exactly when and by whom the files were accessed. In some cases, this requires that individual accounts are in place and that it is clear in the AUP that the individual staff member is responsible for anything that happens with their account whether or not they themselves access the files, etc. In many cases, this allows one to avoid the argument that someone else used the staff member's account. Such subterfuge is fairly rare in reality. It is necessary to determine if any laws were broken and to decide how to involve law enforcement authorities if necessary.

It is also important to ensure that the AUP is not only signed upon a staff member being hired. Some case law requires staff members be regularly reminded of their responsibilities under the AUP. Some districts provide a pop up window each time someone logs in reminding them of the AUP. Other districts provide a memo to all staff annually or more often. If the school does filter staff machines, the staff could argue that since the filter did not stop the said materials, the district inherently approved the materials. That argument needs to be addressed.

A significant issue with regard to any personnel issue is the concept of precedent. Although impossible to determine from the facts in the case, what was done in previous cases. If one staff member was terminated for having logged five hours in an Internet chat room during working hours, someone who logged fifty hours will most likely be terminated. However, if someone only spent fifteen minutes in a chat room, will the district terminate that staff member?

One final issue is that in nearly all personnel actions, the Board of Education usually is the body to terminate and often to suspend. Ensure that if that is the case, one recommends that the employee be terminated instead of telling the person one is terminating them directly. Again, that is a procedural due process that could come back to haunt a school or district.

Mr. Warlick's Videos

The key here is to determine what copyright guidelines allow and ensure that one follows them. Not only does the library media staff need to follow the guidelines, the district should adopt and implement a copyright policy. Notices regarding copyright should be posted on copy machines and other pieces of equipment that can be potentially used to violate copyright.

However, in a school where the culture over time has allowed for the violation of copyright, the staff will need to be provided staff development to explain the law. Staff are often resistant to being told they cannot continue a practice that they have done in the past. Copyright and particularly educational "fair use" is one of the most poorly understood areas of the law. It is important for a school to clearly be able to articulate the actual letter and spirit of the law.

Oh Those Phone Bills

Telephones are an old technology in many ways. However, the telephone is a complicated device. Modern telephone systems allow for a variety of ways to limit access to long distance, international calls, 411, etc. The key is that all phones should be able to dial 911 and other emergency numbers without hindrance. Depending upon the culture of a school, long distance can be routed through an operator or staff needing long distance access can be given PIN numbers to access long distance dialing.

Time of day routing is also important in some cases. Even the superintendent's or principal's offices do not need long distance access after hours. Such phones can be given open access during the day, but restricted in off hours. Often abuse occurs by custodial or security staff on night or weekend shifts when no one is around to supervise. Call logs can be routinely scrutinized to look for calls over 20 minutes or made at odd times of day or night.

What Size Is Your Monitor?

The key to this case is to determine what is a reasonable accommodation. It appears in this particular case the staff member may have an alternative reason for wanting the larger monitor. It is acceptable to do two things in this case. One would be to contact the doctor in question and ask for further clarification. For instance, would resetting the resolution on the monitor be an acceptable accommodation. If one finds that the doctor seems unreasonable or perhaps is a family friend, one can always have the staff member be examined by a doctor of the school's choosing to obtain a second opinion. The second opinion would be at the district's expense however.

To Buy or Not to Buy?

This case is more tightly tied to the potential culture of the district than many. In many districts, the teaching faculty and administration are regularly accorded benefits and opportunities not extended to the non-certified or classified staff. These non-classified staff are also known as educational support personnel (ESPs) and in a current school district most likely include a number of professional positions including the majority of a district's IT staff.

The key to this case is partially in articulating how the district can step back from an implied benefit to one group of staff members while potentially maintaining the benefit for teachers. The simplest answer could be to eliminate the program altogether. Potentially, the past abuses of the system would have to be articulated as to why the past practice would be modified for the future. The culture of the district, as interpreted by the reader should be one of the major considerations in this case regardless of the outcome determined.

The Downloading Blues

This is a key issue for any school districts particularly when technology leadership changes. Each educational technology leader seems to have a different opinion as to the amount of control they wish to have over the activities of the end-users. Many who have progressed through the networking and technical ranks wish to maintain a tighter control than those who came up through the educator ranks. Neither perspective is incorrect. The educator understands the need for flexibility and just in time learning on the part of the teaching faculty. However, flexibility tends to breed inconsistency and a lack of standardization. Standardization is essential in larger schools particularly where machines have to be standardized if the IT staff is to have any hope of being able to support them.

Often teachers will request direct access to load software, but often software programs interact with already installed software causing performance problems. Such access also potentially opens the door to the school or district being liable for copyright problems. This case requires the educational technologist or school library media specialist, who is often caught in the middle on this issue, to balance the needs of the individual teacher against the needs of the system. Any response that does that thoughtfully should work as long as it is clearly communicated to all involved.

To See or Not to See

Again, this case requires a consideration of balance. The needs of the staff development team need to be balanced against the basic security needs of the district. In general, a person's network files should be accessible only by them or those that they feel should have access. For instance, a principal's secretary may have access to the principal's files or a teacher to her aide's files. Even in these cases that seem natural, the principal or teacher aide may not feel comfortable with the arrangement. This becomes more difficult in situations involving e-mail and personnel data as well. General practice tends to be to limit the number of people with access to ALL files on a network or server to only those who require such access to support the servers and the network in general. In many cases, for security reasons, those accounts which do have complete access, often known as "god access," are only used when necessary and those staff members also have a regular ID and password like other end users or at least one that is more limited than full access.

A New Car for the Information Superhighway

The assignment in this case is straightforward. The key to this case is to explain simply and completely all of the points articulated in the assignment. Often parents will seek advice about computer purchasing decisions from the school. It is important that the school be prepared for these inquiries. Being prepared will allow the school to help ensure that home computers and other technologies will likely be compatible with school computers. This ultimately makes life easier for the student that should be a key goal. However, this is not the time to tell the parents to only purchase equipment identical to school equipment. It is important that alternatives be articulated and the system specifications are clearly identified. Name brands and brand loyalty has little place in such recommendations to parents.

Passwords or Spot123

Password and PIN security is a significant issue in today's world. Identify theft is a serious crime. The number of cases continues to grow to the point where credit card companies and banks are airing television commercials to warn consumers of the dangers of identify theft. For whatever reasons, schools tend to have more lax password procedures than other institutions. It is not uncommon to find a teacher using the same password they used five years ago. Dogs' names, children's birthdays, etc. are standard passwords. They are also easy to guess.

In a perfect world, passwords should be changed every month. The same password should not be reused for at least a year. A password should be six to eight characters and not be found in a dictionary. It should also include at least one special character such as an exclamation point, an ampersand or a dollar sign. An easy to remember way to generate passwords is take normal words like apple or blonde and turn them into the passwords @pple! and b!onde$.

Needful Things in the Athletics Office

Although the old boy's network is starting to leave us, in many schools and districts its vestiges still remain. In many schools with significant internal promotions over the years, often administrators and even faculty members whose positions hold little positional authority exercise significant referent power throughout the district.

The key to this case is to articulate the need for standardized data management. The district appears to desire to be more data driven. However, the reticence of the athletic director is causing a great deal of extra work for the MIS staff. One potential solution is to offer the athletic department of Gable High to cover the costs of the additional MIS tasks out of its activity funds. Normally, administrators are hesitant to pay for services that they feel should be free. In addition, it might send a message as to the additional cost of the old way of doing things. If possible, acknowledging any legitimate points made by the athletic director would be wisely politic.

The Vanishing Vendor

This case is one of the most straightforward. The CIO simply needs to articulate the process by which to select a new administrative software program. This requires that the CIO backward plan from the time he or she feels the software will need to be installed. How long will data migration take? Will the new system be run in parallel with the existing system for some time? Will the systems all be migrated at the same time or will student records be given priority for instance? How will the CIO ensure that all stakeholders, including nursing staff, library media specialists, registrars, etc. are including in the decision making process?

One item drawn from experience is that these systems are extremely complicated and often take much longer to migrate to than a salesperson might allude to. Ensuring that the migrated data is clean and accurate is essential. One high school district was unable to print transcripts for nearly three years due to migrating bad data into a new system. Similar issues with payroll systems have literally been the cause of teacher strikes. It is imperative that these processes are well planned and brilliantly executed. Many new systems are much less forgiving of poor record keeping than older systems were.

A Favor for the Boss

This assignment requires that one be able to write questions in such a way as to weave multiple strands into a single question. It is difficult to sit through a long interview where the subject is constantly peppered with specific questions. Better interviews are those that approach the tenor of a conversation. It is difficult to manage this type of an interview, but the results are worth the added preparation. Articulating the questions that need to be asked in both sections of the interview are important. Another key issue is to ensure that the interviewee has the opportunity to ask his or her own questions about the district.

Motivating and Retaining Technical Staff

The case has two primary parts. The first is to determine if the job descriptions are accurate and if they provide enough incentive to keep a young IT staff member involved and interested in the organization. In addition, one must determine what an attractive salary would be for such positions. This will vary widely depending upon the community in which one lives. Finding out what comparable positions in neighboring schools pay is a good place to start. Checking classified ads and speaking with IT recruiting firms might also help in determining reasonable starting salaries.

The second section of the case deals with putting an IT staff development program together for the district. With regard to any staff development program for IT staff, it will need to be personalized not unlike an IEP for special education students. The needs of each IT staff member will tend to be unique, and a programmer and a computer repair person have little in the way of common job skills. Providing access to training for advancing to the next level and providing access to a broad range of training are key ways to keep young IT staff motivated. Often companies give young IT staff members very narrow responsibilities. One of the key advantages of working in an educational environment is the range of software and hardware schools tend to manage. Exploit what is normally a challenge in IT management and make it into a selling point for the IT staff. Ensure that they are given the opportunity to work with a wide variety of programs and equipment. Often young staff can be retained if they see the advantage of working in the school and having the opportunity to gain broader experience than their counterparts in corporate America.

Another facet of retention is to get the IT staff involved in the school community. Where possible get them involved in coaching or sponsoring activities. Often those extra-curricular positions have the ability to bond the employee to the school in a way the job itself is not able to do. Provide opportunities to encourage those activities and develop IT staff relationships with other staff outside of the IT department.

Skills or Else!

The assignment in this case is straightforward. If one's response adequately answers the questions set forth by the superintendent, the assignment will be complete. The key is to balance the need for technology skill with the need to include incentives for the staff to obtain the same. Any response that does not take the ISTE standards into consideration would be remiss.

If phasing standards, one must consider if all new hires are required to meet new standards it could take more than 30 years to reach the entire faculty given the average life cycle of a teaching position. In addition, if standards are phased in, that would potentially set a precedent that all future changes would need to be phased in as well.

Training for the potential standards is essential for success. However, if requiring skills, how will they be assessed and by whom? Unfortunately, those schools that do require and assess technology skills among the teaching staff often spend a great deal of time assessing the staff and developing the assessment itself.

The Managers' Ultimatum

This case clearly illuminates the concept that the most technically proficient still need to be able to get along with others. Often the issues that cause an employee to get into trouble are interpersonal issues and not technical job skills. In this case, the director of technology has to decide how to react to the ultimatum of the other managers. If the director really feels that the other managers may all quit, he or she may react differently than if he or she feels this is a bluff.

Most likely, the network manager needs to be spoken with regarding all of the issues outlined by the other managers. The key question becomes whether or not the ultimatum itself, or even the fact it was offered, is shared with the network manager. Depending upon the situation, the director may or may not want to move quickly in removing the network manager. The key is that the network manager deserves to be accorded due process including the chance to remediate her previous behavior. The situation cannot be ignored, unless the other managers have totally misrepresented the network manager's actions. In nearly any case, there would most likely be some kernel of truth to the managers' representations.

Absentee Teachers in the Labs and Libraries

Flexible scheduling of school library media centers has been an issue since the 1960s. Traditionally, school libraries were a place to drop students off while the teachers took a break or worked with another group of students. That has changed over the past 30 years, but many schools still provide only scheduled library periods in their elementary schools. In the same way, many computer labs are used in the same way, as a time for teacher prep time.

The advantages of using the library and computer resources of a school in a more flexible way have been clearly articulated many times over. However, the issue often becomes the need to maintain the present level of teacher release time and not an issue of what makes the best pedagogical sense. One key to this issue will be to involve the union leadership and ensure they are brought into the conversation early on as well.

Computer Course Requirement

There is little denying that students graduating from high school today should have a rich set of computer skills in order to be prepared for the current and future world of work. The real focus of this case is how should those skills be taught. Should computer skills be taught to students in a special course or should students have to utilize their computer skills across the curriculum? The second course of action is probably the preferred method assuming that all of the teachers in the high school could get together and work out what essential skills were to be taught in each course, etc. The elective nature of the high school curriculum unfortunately hinders such an integrated approach because the very nature of high school curriculum provides for very few courses that all students take. In addition, many high school teachers are still unfortunately either unable or unwilling to provide a strong strand of technology instruction in their courses.

The need to create a separate strand of computer courses does hearken back to other skills in isolation efforts. However, to paraphrase Thomas Jefferson, it might be the best method given the other options that a school has. If a course requirement is required for graduation, some consideration should be given to alternative means of meeting the requirement including a proficiency test or other more advanced coursework.

Going to School At Home?

Online instruction in both asynchronous and synchronous modes is booming in education and in industry. The Virtual High School based in Concord, MA and the Florida Virtual High School both offer legitimate high school coursework throughout the world via the Internet. There is little evidence that seat time makes a better student, but many view online courses or their predecessor tele-courses as less substantial than traditional face-to-face classroom instruction.

The key to this case is to bring some of the research to bear that articulates the benefits of online learning and the fact that nearly every graduate program in the country is trying to define an online course presence if not create entirely online degrees. To ignore online instruction or its potential is akin to the Ludite movement of early industrial England.

Similarly, school districts run a risk of becoming too parochial when they start trying to determine themselves what college or university credits they will accept and what credits they will not accept. If a college offers a three-credit course, the college should stand behind the academic rigor of that course regardless of delivery method. If a university offers a sub-standard online course, isn't there a good chance that college also offers sub-standard classroom instruction as well?

Block Scheduling in the High Schools

Block scheduling does require a fair amount of change from the routines of traditional approximately 45 minute course periods. The key to such change tends to be intensive staff development for the staff during the transition. Few, if any students, will sit for 85 or 90 minutes in a desk and listen to a lecture. Students in block scheduled courses must be more directly engaged in instruction, and a wider range of activities need to be included in the pedagogical milieu of the typical high school.

Two of the activities that tend to be used more often in these longer class periods are computer instruction and library research. Whereas in 45 minutes, the library media specialist can barely get through an introductory lesson and get all of the students to find one or two items, in a block schedule students can have an amount of time conductive to finding materials. However, with fewer periods in day, scheduling classes into the library media center may become slightly more troublesome. Similarly, more teachers will most likely begin to use computer labs since the time it takes to get started and troubleshoot start up problems will take less of the entire class period and students will have more opportunity to actually complete complex assignments.

Depending upon how a specific block schedule is implemented, there many also be a general resource/lunch period in the day which would potentially tax the library media and computer lab resources. So a way of prioritizing students for access to those resources may also have to be considered.

Typing to Graduate

A keyboarding or typing graduation requirement was one of the first types of responses to the need for more technology instruction in high schools. Some of these requirements date from the late 1980s. However, is the ability to type at 20, 25, or even 40 words per minute really an effective measure of a student's grasp of computer productivity concepts? Such a requirement has often been opposed with the argument made in this case. Given such a graduation requirement, how can one work to create a more effective measure of computer proficiency for the school's graduates?

Your Job Is on the Line

This case may be the most difficult to find supporting research for. Very little literature exists around the concept of central or district management of library programs. In addition, many of these jobs and service units are being dissolved and replaced, if at all, by a branch of the technology department. However, just as branch libraries of a pubic or university library system need to adhere to certain systematic standards so must school libraries.

The advantages of centralized guidance and direction for library media specialists and the program in general should be articulated. The potential cost savings and efficiencies of centralized services are also an item to be discussed. Management of district-wide resources such as video libraries and union catalogs need to be conducted by someone. The argument that other district-wide services such as low incidence special education programs and even broader curriculum areas are provided central leadership should be addressed. Why should the art department merit centralized coordination, but the library media program be decentralized? There is more of a need for tight standardization in a library media program than in an art curriculum generally speaking.

To Build or Not to Build: That Is the Question

Unfortunately, the question being asked is not a fictional one. Many schools are looking to disband their computer labs and library media centers in favor of additional classroom resources. Classroom book collections can provide for the leisure reading interests of the students and the Internet can provide all of the research materials needed by a middle school student. At some level, this argument is legitimate. Books and electronic resources in a classroom can provide many of the facts available in the library media center.

However, one would hope that the library media specialist is a value added service. The library media specialist provides students with guidance in the form of readers' advisory and reference help beyond the scope available from one's classroom teacher. The SLMS also provides the classroom teachers guidance and assistance in instructional planning. Similarly, the library media center provides a common space for guided practice whether during study halls and lunch periods or outside of the school day. Maintaining the same level of access to resources without a central library media center would be much more difficult and staff intensive as every teacher would have to be available or students would have to know to go to classrooms other than their own at times.

Library Degree Not Required

This case is similar to the previous case in that the functions of the library media specialist are viewed as the clerical ordering of resources, and the instructional and consultive roles of a certified library media specialist are not being addressed. Surely, a library clerk can open a library media center and check materials in and out. However, who will provide assistance in instructional planning or teach students how to use the resources in the library media center? When those additional responsibilities are articulated, few administrators will continue to want to replace certified library media specialists with clerks. The caveat is that if former school library media specialists only performed the husbanding of materials and their influence did not extend beyond the walls of the library media center or impact the instructional process, it is easy to see how clerical staff might replace them.

The Accountant-less Audit

Auditing technology systems requires looking beyond the boxes and wires that one normally associates with technology. One must look at all aspects of the technology systems that run through a school system in the way mortar runs through a brick building. The bricks are the focus, but without the mortar, the results would be neither functional nor decorative.

The scope of the audit should include all technology systems from the obvious computers, video projectors, and printers to the possibly less obvious telephones, pagers, and copy machines. Do special needs students have access to assistive technologies to help them overcome their disabilities? The audit needs to focus on the interoperability of technology systems as well. Data should be able to move seamlessly between student, financial, and human resource systems. Access to data also needs to be considered.

The organization and management of technology is also important. Is there a clearly defined decision making structure for technology-related issues and has that structure been well communicated throughout the school or district? Are the necessary budgets in place to provide for both the acquisition of new technologies and the support and repair of existing technologies? Are the necessary standards in place to ensure that hardware and software will all function together and not require the IT staff to constantly hurdle unnecessary obstacles?

In short, a technology audit needs to ensure that the district has an organizational structure for technology that enhances technology and does not inhibit the efficient workings of technology within the district. Staff development for technology needs to be systemic. The district needs to have adequate infrastructure resources for current and potentially future needs. Hardware and software need to be standardized and inventoried. The administrative systems need to all work together and share data. All of these systems need to be poised to support the instructional process and provide teachers and administrators resources to be more efficient and effective educators.

The White Elephants

Donations are unfortunately a mixed blessing for schools at times. Often businesses are eager to provide schools with their old computers, printers, etc. This is often as much for a tax break as for philanthropic reasons. These computers often need to be totally rebuilt before being useful to schools if they are to be useful at all.

At the same time, refusing donations can send a bad message especially in a private school that is canvassing the same businesses for other forms of support. Public schools are often in the same situation with booster clubs and educational foundations out canvassing for funds. Care must be taken not to offend, but at the same time white elephant donations are an unnecessary burden on schools. In many cases, accepting out of date computers can cost more in staff time to make the machines work than purchasing new equipment from the start.

Creating a CIO

In effective technology programs, there needs to be centralized leadership. In the same way, a school is often a reflection of its principal; a technology program is a reflection of the CIO. In a school district with a strong administrative CIO, the district will most likely have a strong technology program. Where the technology program is greatly decentralized, the program is much less likely to be on the radar screen of the district's executive leadership.

If a technology program is to be the most effective, it should be holistic and include telephone services, help desk functions, technology staff development, and instructional technology services as well as networking and MIS management. In the strongest programs the library media program and traditional audio-visual services are also included under the umbrella of technology. The library media program often offers a strong avenue for the delivery of educational technology resources and services. Technology programs that need to recreate that delivery avenue on their own are at a significant disadvantage.

Where possible, technology leadership should be centralized at the cabinet level, especially if such is the case with other functional areas within the district such as curriculum and instruction, personnel, or facilities programs. Someone who can speak to the technological impact of all cabinet level decision-making is an asset to any district.

Assessing Your Own District

Assessing technology within a school is very similar to an external audit and the same facets should be considered. Whereas an external audit can only determine where one is and possibly point out deficiencies against local, state, or national standards, an internal assessment should also gauge where one is in relationship to where one would like to be.

The facets that should be considered should include infrastructure (including telephones, network, television, and video distribution), hardware, software, administrative systems, staff readiness, service and support, staff development, integration into the instructional program, technology facilities and the school or district's Internet presence. The assessment should also look to how the district organizes for technology, funds technology, and the policies in place that support technology. One should also review what one feels are the next logical steps for technology growth in each area.

Index

A
Acceptable use policies (AUP) 3, 12, 30, 124
Americans with Disabilities Act (ADA) 27
Audit 106, 124

B
Block scheduling 28, 85, 147-148
Budget and fiscal issues . .vii, 20, 48, 68, 98, 100

C
Case studies
    Facilitation of iv
    Teaching method ii
    Types of iii
Cataloging 94
Chief information officer (CIO) 113, 132, 150
Copyright 7, 36, 139, 141
Curriculum and instruction . . . .v, 3, 10, 146, 148

D
Donations 12, 111

E
Ergonomics . . . . .viii, 27
Evaluation
    Staff 71

F
Facilities . . . . .vi, 97, 151
Faculty and staff concerns 3, 13, 17, 61, 81
Filtering 3-5, 13, 137

H
Home computers 31, 41, 126, 128

I
Intellectual freedom . . . . .ii, 10
    Reconsideration of materials 8, 11
Instructional materials 7-8, 126
    Selection of 10
Instructional technology
    Courses 77
    Online courses .83
    Required skills .87
Internet 3, 13
    Downloading .35
    Pornography 4
Interviews 57

J
Job descriptions 62, 114

L
Leadership . . . . .v, 94, 148, 150
    Facets to consider v
    Teamwork 55, 61, 71
Library programming 85, 93, 97, 101

M
Management information
systems (MIS) 107, 113, 121, 144, 152

N
NET-S 77, 87

P
Parents .8, 41, 137, 142
Passwords .14, 43, 128
Personnel . . . . .vi, 61, 101, 115, 138
Professional development 31, 62, 83
Public relations .vii, 133

T
Technology
    Access to . . . . .viii, 4, 21, 31, 35, 39
    Interoperability . . . . .ix, 149
    Security 14, 36, 43
    Skills .39, 69, 77
    Staff purchase of 31
    Standardization . . . . .ix, 35, 111, 121
    Support of . . . . .ix, 39, 61
Telephone systems . .21, 71, 108, 113, 127, 149, 152

V
Vendors 49, 114, 143
Viruses 36

W
Working conditions 4, 13, 21, 69, 83, 93

www.ingramcontent.com/pod-product-compliance
Lightning Source LLC
Chambersburg PA
CBHW070618300426
44113CB00010B/1571